Literary Criticism

Plato Through Johnson

GOLDENTREE BIBLIOGRAPHIES

In Language and Literature
under the series editorship of
O. B. Hardison, Jr.

Literary Criticism

Plato Through Johnson

compiled by

Vernon Hall

The University of Wisconsin

APPLETON-CENTURY-CROFTS

Educational Division

NewYork MEREDITH CORPORATION

PRINTED IN THE UNITED STATES OF AMERICA
390–40409–8

Preface

UNLIKE MOST of the bibliographies in this series, this one is forced to list a large number of titles in foreign languages. The international nature of literary criticism makes this inevitable. Nevertheless, since this bibliography is designed for intelligent undergraduates as well as graduate students, the bias has been towards publications in English. Wherever an English translation of a foreign work exists, it is included. The arrangement is chronological by period and alphabetical by critic within the period. Works on individual critics follow immediately the works of the critic. A row of asterisks divides the works of the critic from the works about the critic.

In order to keep this bibliography to a practical size, it has been necessary to omit a number of references: unpublished dissertations, literary histories (except for a very few), short notes and explications (except when they contain important data).

In general, the compiler has attempted to steer a middle course between the brief lists of references included in the average textbook and the long professional bibliography in which significant items are often lost in the sheer number of references given. This bibliography should materially assist the student in his effort to survey a topic, write reports and term papers, prepare for examinations, and do independent reading. Attention is called to four features intended to enhance its utility.

(1) Extra margin on each page permits listing of library call numbers of often-used items.

(2) Space at the bottom of every page permits inclusion of additional entries, and blank pages for notes follow the final entry.

(3) An index by author follows the bibliography proper.

(4) The Index and cross-reference numbers direct the reader to the page and position on the page of the desired entry. Thus, in an entry such as

BALDWIN, Charles C. See 3.9.

the number 3.9 indicates that the entry referred to is on page 3 and is the 9th item on that page. Both page numbers and individual entry numbers are conspicuous in size and position so that the process of finding entries is fast as well as simple.

Collections of critical essays which are considered primary source material are listed in a separate section at the beginning of the bibliography. Cross references to works cited in full elsewhere in the bibliography give the author or editor's name, the page, and the location on the page of the entry in question. An asterisk placed after an entry indicates a work of special importance and a dagger that a book is available in a paperback edition. Abbreviations and symbols are those made standard by the *PMLA* annual bibliography except the abbreviations which refer to frequently cited anthologies. The symbols and abbreviations follow, standard *PMLA* symbols listed first and special abbreviations second.

AFMag	Annali della Facoltà di Magistero (U of Palermo)
AJP	American Journal of Philology
APh	Acta Philologica (Roma: Societas Academica Daco-romana)
ARS	Augustan Reprint Society
BFM	Boletín de Filología (Montevideo)
BHR	Bibliothèque d'Humanisme et Renaissance
BJA	British Journal of Aesthetics
BJRL	Bulletin of the John Rylands Library
BNYPL	Bulletin of the New York Public Library
BuR	Bucknell Review
CaiSE	Cairo Studies in English
CE	College English
CEA	CEA Critic
CJ	Classical Journal
CL	Comparative Literature
CRAS	The Centennial Review of Arts and Science
CSE	Cornell Studies in English
CW	Classical World
DA	Dissertation Abstracts
DramS	Drama Survey
DSS	XVIIième Siècle
EA	Études Anglaises

E&S	Essays and Studies
ECr	L'Esprit Créateur (Lawrence, Kansas)
EIC	Essays in Criticism
ELH	Journal of English Literary History
ES	English Studies
ESMEA	Essays and Studies by Members of the English Association
Expl	Explicator
FeL	Filologia e Letteratura
FMLS	Forum for Modern Language Studies
FR	French Review
FS	French Studies
GCFI	Giornale Critico della Filosophia Italiana
GSLI	Giornale Storico della Letteratura Italiana
HLQ	Huntington Library Quarterly
HSCP	Harvard Studies in Classical Philology
HudR	Hudson Review
IJES	Indian Journal of English Studies (Calcutta)
IL	L'Information Littéraire
ISLL	Illinois Studies in Language and Literature
IUPHS	Indiana University Publications, Humanistic Series
JAAC	Journal of Aesthetics and Art Criticism
JBS	Journal of British Studies
JEGP	Journal of English and Germanic Philology
JGE	Journal of General Education
JHI	Journal of the History of Ideas
JS	Journal des Savants
JWCI	Journal of the Warburg and Courtauld Institute
KR	Kenyon Review
LLA	Library of Liberal Arts
LM	Language Monographs
LT	Levende Talen
MCR	Melbourne Critical Review
MLN	Modern Language Notes
MLQ	Modern Language Quarterly
MLR	Modern Language Review
MP	Modern Philology
N&Q	Notes and Queries
NLB	Newberry Library Bulletin
NRam	New Rambler (Johnson Society, London)
NS	Die Neueren Sprachen
NSch	New Scholasticism
PBA	Proceedings of the British Academy
PhQ	Philosophical Quarterly
PhR	Philosophical Review
PLL	Papers on Language and Literature
PMASAL	Papers of the Michigan Academy of Science, Arts, and Letters
PMLA	Publications of the Modern Language Association
PPR	Philosophy and Phenomenological Research
PQ	Philological Quarterly

QJS	Quarterly Journal of Speech
RBPH	Revue Belge de Philologie et d'Histoire
RdE	Revista di Estetica (U of Padua)
RECTR	Restoration and 18th Century Theatre Research
REL	Review of English Literature
RenP	Renaissance Papers
RES	Review of English Studies
RF	Romanische Forschungen
RIPh	Review Internationale de Philosophie (Brussels)
RLI	Rassengna della Letteratura Italiana
RLMC	Rivista di Letterature Moderne e Comparate (Florence)
RMM	Revue de Métaphysique et de Morale
RR	Romanic Review
SB	Studies in Bibliography
SCN	Seventeenth-Century Notes
SEL	Studies in English Literature, 1500–1900
SF&R	Scholars' Facsimiles and Reprints
SFI	Studi di Filologia Italiana
SFr	Studi Francesi
SGG	Studia Germanica Gandensia
SM	Speech Monographs
SN	Studia Neophilologica
SÖAW	Sitzungsberichte der Österreichischen Akademie der Wissenschaften in Wien. Phil.-Hist. Klasse
SoQ	The Southern Quarterly (U of So. Mississippi)
SP	Studies in Philology
SQ	Shakespeare Quarterly
SR	Sewanee Review
SRen	Studies in the Renaissance
SSe	Studi Secenteschi
SSJ	Southern Speech Journal
SSL	Studies in Scottish Literature
SSLL	Stanford Studies in Language and Literature
ST	Studi Tassiani
StI	Studi Italiani
SWR	Southwest Review
TLS	Times Literary Supplement (London)
TSL	Tennessee Studies in Literature
TSLL	Texas Studies in Literature and Language
UCDPE	University of California at Davis, Publications in English
UGM	University of Georgia Monographs
UNCSRLL	University of North Carolina Studies in Romance Languages and Literatures
UTET	Unione Tipografico–Editrice Torinese
UTQ	University of Toronto Quarterly
VLit	Voprosy Literatury
XUS	Xavier University Studies
YSE	Yale Studies in English
ZFSL	Zeitschrift für Französische Sprache und Literatur

Special abbreviations for frequently cited anthologies:

C&C	R. S. Crane, ed., *Critics and Criticism.* See 4.4.
CEEC	W. H. Durham, ed., *Critical Essays of the 18th Century.* See 1.11.
CESC	J. E. Spingarn, ed., *Critical Essays of the 17th Century.* See 2.15.
CM	S. Elledge and D. Schier, eds., *The Continental Model.* See. 1.13.
CP	B. Weinberg, ed., *Critical Prefaces of the French Renaissance.* See 2.17.
ECCE	S. Elledge, ed., *Eighteenth-Century Critical Essays.* See 1.12.
ECE	G. G. Smith, ed., *Elizabethan Critical Essays.* See 2.13.
ELC	S. Hynes, ed., *English Literary Criticism.* See 2.3.
GC	J. H. Smith and E. W. Parks, eds., *The Great Critics.* See 2.14.
LC	A. H. Gilbert, ed., *Literary Criticism: Plato to Dryden.* See 1.17.

I should like to acknowledge the kind assistance of John O. Hayden of the University of California at Davis, my colleagues Gian Orsini, Peter Boerner, Fanny LeMoine, and Gene Rister, and my wife, Sandra.

Note: The publisher and compiler invite suggestions for additions to future editions of this bibliography.

Contents

Later Criticism Through Johnson

CONTENTS

CONTENTS

Collections of Critical Essays

1   ADAMS, Henry Hitch, and Baxter HATHAWAY, eds. *Dramatic Essays of the Neoclassical Age*. New York: Columbia U P, 1950.

2   AGATE, James E., ed. *The English Dramatic Critics: An Anthology, 1660–1932*. New York: Hill and Wang, 1958.

3   BATE, Walter Jackson, ed. *Criticism: The Major Texts*. New York: Harcourt, Brace, 1952.

4   BATESON, Frederick Wilse, ed. *Essays in Criticism*. N.p., 1951.

5   BIGI, Emilio, ed. *Dal Muratori al Cesarotti*. Milan: Ricciardi, 1960.

6   CHAPMAN, Gerald Wester, ed. *Literary Criticism in England, 1660–1800*. New York: Knopf, 1966.

7   COOK, Albert S., ed. *The Art of Poetry: The Poetical Treatises of Horace, Vida, and Boileau, with the Translations by Howes, Pitt, and Soame*. Boston: Ginn, 1926.

8   DENNISTON, John Dewar, ed. and trans. *Greek Literary Criticism*. New York: Dutton, 1924.

9   DODDS, E. R., ed. and trans. *Select Passages Illustrating Neoplatonism*. New York: Macmillan, 1923.

10   DORSCH, T. S., ed. and trans. *Classical Literary Criticism*. Baltimore: Penguin, 1965. [L155]†

11   DURHAM, Willard Higley, ed. *Critical Essays of the 18th Century*. New York: Russell and Russell, 1961.

12   ELLEDGE, Scott, ed. *Eighteenth-Century Critical Essays*. 2 vols. Ithaca: Cornell U P, 1960.

13   ———, and Donald SCHIER, eds. *The Continental Model: Selected French Critical Essays of the Seventeenth Century in English Translation*. Minneapolis: Carleton Col, 1960.

14   ENRIGHT, Dennis Joseph, and Ernst DE CHICHERA, eds. *English Critical Texts, 16th Century to 20th Century*. London: Oxford U P, 1962.

15   Fyfe, W. H., and W. R. ROBERTS, eds. and trans. *Aristotle: The Poetics, Longinus: On the Sublime, Demetrius: On Style*. New York: Putnam, 1927. [Loeb ed.]

16   GEBERT, Clara, ed. *An Anthology of Elizabethan Dedications and Prefaces*. Philadelphia: U of Pennsylvania P, 1933.

17   GILBERT, Allan H., ed. *Literary Criticism: Plato to Dryden*. New York: American Book, 1940. [WB1]† [All English.]

18   HALM, Karl von, ed. *Rhetores Latini Minores*. Leipzig, 1863.

19   HARDISON, O. B., Jr., ed. *English Literary Criticism: The Renaissance*. New York: Appleton-Century-Crofts, 1963.

1   HASLEWOOD, Joseph, ed. *Ancient Critical Essays upon English Poets and Poesy.* 2 vols. London: Triphook, 1811–15.

2   HOLMES, Charles S., Edwin FUSSELL, and Ray FRAZER, eds. *The Major Critics: The Development of English Literary Criticism.* New York: Knopf, 1965.

3   HYNES, Samuel, ed. *English Literary Criticism: Restoration and 18th Century.* London: Owen, 1964. [Appleton]†

4   JONES, Edmund David, ed. *English Critical Essays (Sixteenth, Seventeenth, and Eighteenth Centuries).* London: Oxford U P, 1961.

5   KAPLAN, Charles, ed. *Criticism: Twenty Major Statements.* San Francisco: Chandler, n.d.

6   KRAUSS, Werner, and Hans KORTUM, eds. *Antike und Moderne in der Literaturdiskussion des 18. Jahrhunderts.* Berlin: Akademie, 1966.

7   LOFTIS, John, ed. *Essays on the Theatre from 18th-Century Periodicals.* Los Angeles: Clark Memorial Library, U.C.L.A., 1960.

8   OXENHANDLER, Neal, ed. *French Literary Criticism: The Basis of Judgment.* Englewood Cliffs, N.J.: Prentice-Hall, 1966.

9   PETRONIO, Giuseppe, ed. *Antologia della critica letteraria.* II: *Dal neoclassicismo al decadentismo.* 4th ed. Bari: Laterza, 1966.

10   SCHORER, Mark, et al., eds. *Criticism: The Foundations of Modern Literary Judgment.* Rev. ed. New York: Harcourt, Brace, 1958.

11   SESONSKE, Alexander, ed. *What Is Art? Aesthetic Theory from Plato to Tolstoy.* New York: Oxford U P, 1965.

12   SMITH, David Nichol, ed. *Eighteenth-Century Essays on Shakespeare.* Glasgow: MacLehose, 1903.

13   SMITH, George Gregory, ed. *Elizabethan Critical Essays.* 2 vols. Oxford: Oxford U P, 1959.

14   SMITH, James Harry, and E. W. PARKS, eds. *The Great Critics.* 3rd ed. rev. and enl. New York: Norton, 1951.

15   SPINGARN, Joel Elias, ed. *Critical Essays of the 17th Century.* 3 vols. Bloomington: Indiana U P, 1963. [Italian edition, see 27.7.]

16   TAYLER, Edward William, ed. *Literary Criticism of the Seventeenth Century.* New York: Knopf, 1967.

17   WEINBERG, Bernard, ed. *Critical Prefaces of the French Renaissance.* Evanston: Northwestern U P, 1950.

General Works

18   ABBOTT, C. C. "Rhetoric and Literary Form." *QJS*, 36 (1950):457–61.

1 ABRAMS, Meyer Howard. *The Mirror and the Lamp*. New York: Oxford U P, 1953. [Norton-N102.]*†

2 AGAR, Herbert. *Milton and Plato*. Princeton: Princeton U P, 1928.

3 ARTHOS, John. *Dante, Michelangelo and Milton*. London: Routledge and Kegan Paul, 1963.

4 ATKINS, John William Hey. *English Literature Criticism*. 3 vols. I: *The Medieval Phase*. Cambridge: U P, 1943; II: *The Renascence*. London: Methuen, 1947; III: *The Seventeenth and Eighteenth Centuries*. London: Methuen, 1951. [175-U P. B&N.]*†

5 AUERBACH, Erich. *Literatursprache und Publikum in der lateinischen Spätantike und im Mittelalter*. Bern: Francke, 1958. [*Literary Language and Its Public in Late Latin Antiquity and in the Middle Ages*, trans. Ralph Manheim. London: Routledge and Kegan Paul, 1965.]

6 ———. *Mimesis*. Bern: Francke, 1946.* [Trans. Willard Trask. Garden City, N.Y.: Doubleday, 1957. (Anchor-A107)†]

7 BACCI, Orazio. *La Critica letteraria (dall' antichità classica al rinascimento)*. Milan: Vallardi, 1910.

8 BALDENSPERGER, Fernand, and Werner P. FRIEDERICH. *Bibliography of Comparative Literature*. New York: Russell and Russell, 1960.

9 BALDWIN, Charles Sears. *Ancient Rhetoric and Poetic, Interpreted from Representative Works*. Gloucester, Mass.: Smith, 1959.

10 BEARDSLEY, Monroe C. *Aesthetics from Classical Greece to the Present: A Short History*. New York: Macmillan, 1966.*

11 BECKSON, Karl E. *Great Theories in Literary Criticism*. New York: Farrar, Straus, 1963. [Noonday-N241.]†

12 BEHRENS, Irene. *Die Lehre von der Einteilung der Dichtkunst, vornehmlich vom 16. bis 19. Jahrhundert: Studien zur Geschichte der poetischen Gattungen*. Halle: Niemeyer, 1940.

13 BORINSKI, Karl. *Die Antike in Poetik und Kunsttheorie vom Ausgang des klassischen Altertums bis auf Goethe und Wilhelm von Humboldt*. 2 vols. Leipzig: Dieterich, 1914–24.*

14 BOSANQUET, Bernard. *A History of Aesthetic*. New York: Macmillan, 1892.

15 BOYD, J. D. *The Function of Mimesis and Its Decline*. Cambridge, Mass.: Harvard U P, 1968.

16 BROCKRIEDE, Wayne E. "Toward a Contemporary Aristotelian Theory of Rhetoric." *QJS*, 52:33–40.

17 BRYAN, Robert Armistead. "The Reputation of John Donne in England from 1600 to 1832: A Study in the History of Literary Criticism." *DA*, 21:2702–3.

18 BRYANT, Donald Cross, ed. *Papers in Rhetoric and Poetic: Presented at the University of Iowa, November 12 and 13, 1964*. Iowa City: U of Iowa P, 1965.

1 BUNDY, Murray Wright. *Theory of Imagination in Classical and Medieval Thought*. Urbana: U of Illinois P, 1927. [ISLL, 12, nos. 2–3.]

2 CARRITT, Edgar Frederick. *Philosophies of Beauty from Socrates to Robert Bridges*. Oxford: Clarendon P, 1931.

3 CLARK, Donald Lemen. "Ancient Rhetoric and English Renaissance Literature." *SQ*, 2 (1951):195–204.

4 CRANE, Ronald S., ed. *Critics and Criticism: Ancient and Modern*. Chicago: U of Chicago P, 1957. [Phoenix. P15]†

5 CROCE, Benedetto. *Estetica come scienza dell'espressione e linguistica generale*. Milan: Sandron, 1902. [*Aesthetic as Science of Expression and General Linguistic*, trans. Douglas Ainslie. 2d ed. London: Macmillan, 1922.*]

6 ———. *La Poesia: Introduzione alla criticà e storia e della letteratura*. Bari: Laterza, 1936. [No English translation.]

7 CUNNINGHAM, James Vincent. *Tradition and Poetic Structure: Essays in Literary History and Criticism*. Denver: Swallow, 1960.

8 DAICHES, David. *Critical Approaches to Literature*. Englewood Cliffs, N.J.: Prentice-Hall, 1956. [Norton]†

9 DAVIES, Cicely. "Ut Pictura Poesis." *MLR*, 30 (1935):159–69.

10 DWIVEDI, Ram Awadh, and Vikramaditya RAI. *Literary Criticism*. Delhi: Motilal Banarsidass, 1965.

11 ELIOT, T. S. *Use of Poetry and the Use of Criticism: Studies in the Relation of Criticism to Poetry in England*. Cambridge, Mass.: Harvard U P, 1933.

12 FERNÁNDEZ Y GONZÁLEZ, Francisco. *Historia de la critica literaria en España*. 5 vols. Madrid: Gomez Fuentenebro, 1867.

13 FIGUEIREDO, F. de. *Historia da critica literaria em Portugal da renascença á actualidade*. Lisbon: Teixeira, 1916.

14 FUBINI, Mario. *Stile, linguaggio, poesia: Considerazioni sulla critica letteraria*. Milan: Marzorati, 1948.

15 GETTO, Giovani. *Letteratura e critica nel tempo*. Milan: Marzorati, 1954.

16 GILBERT, Katherine E., and Helmut KUHN. *A History of Esthetics*. New York: Macmillan, 1939.

17 GILLET, Joseph E. "The Vogue of Literary Theories in Germany from 1500 to 1730." *MP*, 14 (1916–17):341–56.

18 GOAD, Caroline Mabel. *Horace in the English Literature of the Eighteenth Century*. New Haven: Yale U P, 1918.

19 GREENE, Theodore M. *The Arts and the Art of Criticism*. 2d ed. Princeton: Princeton U P, 1947.

20 GRUCKER, Émile. *Historie des doctrines littéraires et esthétique en Allemagne*. Paris, 1883.

21 HACK, Roy Kenneth. "The Doctrine of Literary Forms." *Harvard Studies in Classical Philology*, 27 (1916):35–36.

1   HALL, Lawrence Sargent, ed. *A Grammar of Literary Criticism: Essays in Definition of Vocabulary, Concepts, and Aims.* New York: Macmillan, 1965.

2   HALL, Vernon. *A Short History of Literary Criticism.* New York: New York U P, 1963. [NYU]*†

3   HATZFELD, Helmut. "Three National Deformations of Aristotle: Tesauro, Gracián, Boileau." *SSe*, 2 (1961):3–21.

4   HENN, Thomas Rice. *Longinus and English Criticism.* Cambridge: U P, 1934.

5   HERRICK, Marvin T. *Tragicomedy: Its Origin and Development in Italy, France and England.* Urbana: U of Illinois P, 1962.

6   HOWARD, William G. "Ut Pictura Poesis." *PMLA*, 14 (1909):46–123.

7   KITTO, H. D. F. "Catharsis." In *The Classical Tradition: Literary and Historical Studies in Honor of Harry Caplan*, ed. Wallach Luitpold. Ithaca: Cornell U P , 1966, pp. 133–47.

8   KOMMERELL, Max. *Lessing und Aristoteles: Untersuchung über die Theorie der Tragödie.* Frankfurt: Klostermann, 1957.

9   KRISTELLER, Paul O. "The Modern System of the Arts: A Study in the History of Aesthetics." *JHI*, 12 (1951):496–527.*

10 LANSON, Gustave. "Sur l'influence de la philosophie cartesienne sur la littérature française." *RMM*, 4:517–50.

11 McKEON, Richard. "Imitation and Poetry." In his *Thought, Action, and Passion.* Chicago: U of Chicago P, 1954.

12 MARKWARDT, Bruno. *Geschichte der deutschen Poetik.* Berlin: De Gruyter, 1937–59.

13 MENÉNDEZ Y PELAYO, Marcelino. *Historia de las ideas estéticas en España.* 5 vols. 3d ed. rev. and collated by D. Enrique Sánchez Reyes. Madrid: Consejo Superior de Investigaciones Cientifícas, 1962.*

14 MOMIGLIANO, Attilio. *Problemi ed orientamenti critici di lingua e di letteratura italiana.* 5 vols. Milan: Marzorati, 1948–59.

15 MONTGOMERY, Robert L., Jr. "Allegory and the Incredible Fable: The Italian View from Dante to Tasso." *PMLA*, 81(1966):45–55.

16 MOREAU, Pierre. *La Critique littéraire en France.* Paris: Colin, 1960.

17 MORIER, Henry. *Dictionnaire de poétique et de rhétorique.* 1st ed. Paris: P U de France, 1961.

18 NORDEN, Eduard. *Die antike Kunstprosa vom VI. Jahrhundert v. Chr. bis in die Zeit der Renaissance.* 2 vols. Leipzig, 1898.*

19 OLSON, Elder. "An Outline of Poetic Theory." *C&C*, pp. 546–66.

20 OLZIEN, Otto. *Bibliographie zur deutschen Literaturgeschichte.* Stuttgart: Metzler, 1953.

1 PADELFORD, Frederick Morgan, ed. *Essays on the Study and Use of Poetry.* New York: Holt, 1902. [YSE, 15]

2 PATTERSON, W. F. *Three Centuries of French Poetic Theory: A Critical History of the Chief Arts of Poetry in France, 1328–1630.* 3 vols. New York: Russell and Russell, 1966.

3 PREMINGER, Alex, ed., asso. eds. Frank J. WARNKE and O. B. HARDISON, Jr. *Encyclopedia of Poetry and Poetics.* Princeton: Princeton U P, 1965.*

4 PRITCHARD, John Paul. "Horace's Influence upon American Criticism." *Transactions and Proceedings of the American Philological Association,* 67(1937):228–62.

5 ———. *Return to the Fountains: Some Classical Sources of American Criticism.* Durham: Duke U P, 1942.

6 QUINLAN, M. A. *Poetic Justice in the Drama.* Notre Dame, Ind.: Notre Dame U P, 1912.

7 RANSOM, John Crowe. *The World's Body.* New York: Scribner's, 1938. [Louisiana State U P-L28]*†

8 ROGERSON, Brewster. "The Art of Painting the Passions." *JHI,* 14(1953): 68–94.

9 ROUTH, James Edward. *The Rise of Classical English Criticism: A History of the Canons of English Literary Taste and Rhetorical Doctrine, from the Beginning of English Criticism to the Death of Dryden.* New Orleans: Tulane U P, 1915.

10 SAINTSBURY, George. *A History of Criticism and Literary Taste in Europe* 3 vols. Edinburgh: Blackwood, 1949.*

11 ———. *A History of English Criticism.* Rev., adapted, and supp. ed. Edinburgh: Blackwood, 1962.

12 SANDYS, Sir John Edwin. *A History of Classical Scholarship.* 3 vols. Cambridge: U P, 1921.

13 SEIDEL, George J. *The Crisis of Creativity.* Notre Dame, Ind.: Notre Dame U P, 1966.

14 SHIPLEY, Joseph T., ed. *Dictionary of World Literature: Criticism—Forms—Technique.* New York: Philosophical Library, 1943. [Littlefield-135]†

15 STEADMAN, John M. "Chaste Muse and 'Casta Juventus': Milton Minturno, and Scaliger on Inspiration and the Poet's Character." *Italica,* 40 (1963):28–34.

16 SWEDENBERG, Hugh Thomas, Jr. *The Theory of the Epic in England, 1650–1800.* Berkeley: U of California P, 1944.

17 TATE, Allen. "Longinus and the 'New Criticism.'" In his *The Forlorn Demon: Didactic and Critical Essays.* Chicago: Regnery, 1953.

18 THOMAS, P. G. *Aspects of Literary Theory and Practice, 1550–1870.* London: Heath, Cranton, 1931.

19 TRABALZA, Ciro. *La Critica letteraria (dai primordi dell' umanesimo all' età nostra).* Milan: Vallardi, 1915. [A continuation of Orazio Bacci's *La Critica letteraria (dall' antichità classica al rinascimento).*]

1 TROWBRIDGE, Hoyt. "Aristotle and the New Criticism." *SR*, 52:537–55.

2 WADSWORTH, Philip A. "A Formula of Literary Criticism from Aristotle to La Bruyère." *MLQ*, 7:35–42.

3 WATSON, George. *The Literary Critics: A Study of English Descriptive Criticism.* New York: Barnes and Noble, 1964.

4 WELLEK, René. *Concepts of Criticism*, ed. S. G. Nichols, Jr. New Haven: Yale U P, 1963. [Y86]†

5 ———. *The Rise of English Literary History.* Chapel Hill: U of North Carolina P, 1941.

6 ———, and Austin WARREN. *Theory of Literature.* New York: Harcourt, Brace, 1949. [Harvest. HB75]*†

7 WILCOX, John. "The Beginnings of 'l'Art pour l'Art.'" *JAAC*, 11(1953):360–77.

8 WIMSATT, William K. *The Verbal Icon.* Lexington: U of Kentucky P, 1954. [111]†

9 ———, and Cleanth BROOKS. *Literary Criticism: A Short History.* New York: Knopf, 1965. [1957]*

10 ZUPNICK, I. L. "The 'Aesthetics' of the Early Mannerists." *Art Bulletin*, 25:302–6.

Classical Criticism

General

11 ARBUSOW, Leonid. *Colores Rhetorici.* Göttingen: Vandenhoeck & Ruprecht, 1963.

12 ATKINS, John William Hey. *Literary Criticism in Antiquity.* 2 vols. Cambridge: U P, 1934.*

13 BALDWIN, Charles Sears. See 3.9.

14 BOWRA, C. M. *Sophoclean Tragedy.* Oxford: Clarendon P, 1944. [OX96]†

15 BOYD, John D. See 3.15.

16 BUTCHER, Samuel Henry. *Harvard Lectures on the Originality of Greece.* London: Macmillan, 1911. [First printed as *Harvard Lectures on Greek Subjects*, 1904.]

17 CHAMBERS, Frank Pentland. *Cycles of Taste: An Unacknowledged Problem in Ancient Art and Criticism.* Cambridge, Mass.: Harvard U P, 1928.

18 CLARK, Donald Lemen. "Imitation: Theory and Practice in Roman Rhetoric." *QJS*, 37(1951):11–12.

19 CLARKE, Martin Lowther. *Rhetoric at Rome: A Historical Survey.* London: Cohen & West, 1953.

1   COOPER, Lane. "The Villain as 'Hero.'" In his *Aristotelian Papers.* Ithaca: Cornell U P, 1939.

2   CURTIUS, E. R. "Antike Rhetorik und vergleichende Literaturwissenschaft." *CL*, 1(1949):24–43.

3   D'ALTON, John Francis. *Roman Literary Theory and Criticism.* New York: Longmans, Green, 1931.

4   DENNISTON, John Dewar. See 1.8.

5   DESMOULIEZ, A. "La Signification esthétique des comparaisons entre le style et le corps humain dans la rhétorique antique." *REL*, 33(1955):59ff.

6   DONOHUE, James John. *The Theory of Literary Kinds: Ancient Classifications of Literature.* Dubuque: Loras Col P, 1943.

7   DORSCH, T. S. See 1.10.

8   ELSE, Gerald Frank. "Imitation in the Fifth Century," *Classical Philology*, 53(1958), 73–90.

9   FISKE, George Converse. *Lucilius and Horace: A Study in the Classical Theory of Imitation.* Madison: U of Wisconsin P, 1920. [University of Wisconsin Studies in Language and Literature, 7.]

10   ———, and Mary A. GRANT. *Cicero's "De Oratore" and Horace's "Ars Poetica."* Madison: U of Wisconsin P, 1929. [University of Wisconsin Studies in Language and Literature, 27.]

11   GILBERT, Allan H., and Henry L. SNUGGS. "On the Relation of Horace to Aristotle in Literary Criticism." *JEGP*, 47(1947):233–47.

12   GIOVANNI, G. "The Connection Between Tragedy and History in Ancient Criticism." *PQ*, 22:611–21.

13   GOMME, Arnold Wycombe. *The Greek Attitude to Poetry and History.* Berkeley: U of California P, 1954.

14   GREENE, W. C. "The Greek Criticism of Poetry: A Reconsideration." In *Perspectives of Criticism*, ed. Harry Levin. Cambridge, Mass.: Harvard U P, 1950. pp. 19–53.

15   GRUBE, Georges Maximilien Antoine. *The Greek and Roman Critics.* London: Methuen, 1965. [U of Toronto P 72]*†

16   ———. "Three Greek Critics." *UTQ* 21(1952), 345–61.

17   HERRICK, Marvin T. *The Fusion of Horatian and Aristotelian Literary Criticism, 1531–1555.* Urbana: University of Illinois, 1946. [*ISLL*, 32, no. 1.]

18   JONES, Henry John Franklin. *On Aristotle and Greek Tragedy.* New York: Oxford U P, 1962. [228]*†

19   KENNEDY, George. *The Art of Persuasion in Greece.* Princeton: Princeton U P, 1964.

20   KROLL, Wilhelm. "Rhetorik." *Pauly-Wissowa, Real-Encyclopädie der classischen Altertumswissenschaft.* Stuttgart: Metzler, 1894–1919. Supplement, 7(1940):1039–139.

21   LELIÈVRE, F. J. "The Basis of Ancient Parody." *Greece and Rome*, n.s. 1(1954):66–81.

22   LESKY, Albin. *Geschichte der griechischen Literatur.* Bern: Francke, 1957–58. [*A History of Greek Literature*, trans. James Willis and Cornelius de Heer. London: Methuen, 1966.]

23   McKEON, Richard. "Literary Criticism and the Concept of Imitation in Antiquity." *C&C*, pp. 147–75.

1 ———. "The Philosophic Bases of Art and Criticism. *C&C*, pp. 463–545.

2 NORTH, Helen. "The Use of Poetry in the Education of the Ancient Orator." *Traditio*, 8(1952):1–33.

3 PLEBE, Armando. *La Teoria del comico da Aristotele a Plutarco*. Torino: University of Turin, Faculty of Literature and Philosophy, 1952.

4 RAINES, J. M. "Comedy and the Comic Poets in the Greek Epigram. *Transactions and Proceedings of the American Philological Association*, 77(1946):83–102.

5 ROBERTS, William Rhys. *Greek Rhetoric and Literary Theory*. New York: Longmans, Green, 1928.

6 ROSTAGNI, Augusto. "Aristotele e aristotelismo nella storia dell'estetica antica." In his *Scritti Minori*. 2 vols. Turin: Bottega d'Erasmo, 1955. 1:76–254.*

7 SIKES, Edward Ernest. *The Greek View of Poetry*. London: Methuen, 1923.

8 ———. *Roman Poetry*. London: Methuen, 1923.

9 SOLMSEN, Friedrich. "The Aristotelian Tradition in Ancient Rhetoric." *AJP*, 62(1941):35–50:169–90.

10 WARRY, J. G. *Greek Aesthetic Theory: A Study of Callistic and Aesthetic Concepts in the Works of Plato and Aristotle*. New York: Barnes and Noble, 1962.

Individual Authors

Aristotle

11 *Aristotle on the Art of Fiction*, trans. Leonard James Potts. Cambridge: U P, 1953. Gordian-Sbn. 521 09551 4]

12 *Aristotle on the Art of Poetry*, trans. Ingram Bywater. Oxford: Clarendon P, 1909.

13 *Aristotle: Poetics*, trans. Gerald F. Else. Ann Arbor: U of Michigan P, 1967.

14 *Aristotle: The Poetics*. See 1.15.

15 *Aristotle's Poetics: A Translation and Commentary For Students of Literature*, trans. Leon Golden, commentary O. B. Hardison, Jr. Englewood Cliffs, N.J.: Prentice-Hall, 1968.

16 *Aristotle's Theory of Poetry and Fine Art*, trans. Samuel Henry Butcher. London: Macmillan, 1932. [Dover]†

17 *The "Art" of Rhetoric*, trans. John Henry Freese. New York: Putnam, 1926.

18 *La Poetica di Aristotele*, ed. and commentary Augusto Rostagni. Turin: Chiantore, 1934.

19 *Poetics*, ed. and commentary D. W. Lucas. London: Oxford U P, 1968.

20 *Rhetoric*, trans. Sir Richard Claverhouse Jebb. Cambridge: U P, 1909.

21 *The Works of Aristotle*, trans. under the direction of eds. J. A. Smith and W. D. Ross. 12 vols. Oxford: Clarendon P, 1908–52.

*   *   *

1 AVERROES-HERMANUS Alemannus. See 21.14.

2 BRÉMOND, Henri. "Aristote et la poésie dépoétisée," in his *Prière et poésie*. Paris: Grasset, 1926.

3 CERRETA, Florindo V. "Allessandro Piccolomini's Commentary on the *Poetics* of Aristotle." *SRen*, 4:139–68.

4 COLLINS, J. "Aristotle's Philosophy of Art and the Beautiful." *New Scholasticism*, 16:257–84.

5 COOPER, Lane. *An Aristotelian Theory of Comedy*. New York: Harcourt, Brace, 1922.

6 ———. "Ἁμαρτία Again—AND AGAIN." *CJ*, 33:39–40.

7 ———. *A Bibliography of the Poetics of Aristotle*. New Haven: Yale U P, 1928.* [See Else, Gerald F. "Survey of Works . . . ," 10.11, and Herrick, Marvin T. "A Supplement . . . ," 10.19]

8 ———. *The Poetics of Aristotle: Its Meaning and Influence*. Boston: Marshall Jones, 1923.

9 ———. "The Verbal 'Ornament' (Kosmos) in Aristotle's Art of Poetry." In *Classical and Medieval Studies in Honor of Edward Kennard Rand*, ed. Leslie W. Jones. New York: The Editor, 1938, pp. 61–77.

10 ELSE, Gerald F. *Aristotle's Poetics: The Argument*. Cambridge, Mass.: Harvard U P, 1957.*

11 ———. "Survey of Work on Aristotle's *Poetics*, 1940–1954." *CW*, 48(1954–55):73–82.

12 FLYNN, Lawrence J. "Aristotle: Art and Faculty of Rhetoric." *SSJ*, 21:244–54.

13 GEARHART, Sally Miller. "Aristotle and Modern Theorists on Elements of Tragedy." *DA*, 17:429 (Ill).

14 GILBERT, Allan H. "The Aristotelian Catharsis." *PhR*, 35(1926):301–14.

15 ———. "Aristotle's Four Species of Tragedy and Their Importance for Dramatic Criticism." *AJP*, 68:363–81.

16 ———. "Aristotle's τὸν ὅμοιον (Poetics 13.53 a 5)." *SP*, 56(1959):1–6.

17 GILBERT, Katharine E. "Aesthetic Imitation and Imitators in Aristotle." *PhR*, 45(1936):558–73.

18 HARDISON, O. B. and Leon Golder. See 9.13.

19 HARSH, Philip Whaley. "Ἁμαρτία Again." *Transactions and Proceedings of the American Philological Association*, 76(1945):47–58.

20 HERRICK, Marvin Theodore. *The Poetics of Aristotle in England*. New Haven: Published for Cornell U by Yale U P, 1930.*

21 ———. "A Supplement to Cooper and Gudeman's Bibliography of the *Poetics* of Aristotle." *AJP*, 52(1931):168–74.

22 House, Humphrey. *Aristotle's Poetics: A Course of Eight Lectures*. London Hart-Davis, 1956.*

1   JONES, Henry John Franklin. See 8.16.*

2   LOCK, Walter. "The Use of περιπέτεια in Aristotle's *Poetics*." *Classical Review*, 9(1895):251–53.

3   LUCAS, D. W. See 9.19.

4   LUCAS, Frank Laurence. "The Reverse of Aristotle." *Classical Review*, 37(1923):98–104.

5   ——. *Tragedy: Serious Drama in Relation to Aristotle's Poetics*. Rev. ed New York: Collier, 1962. [01246]*†

6   McBURNEY, James H. "Some Recent Interpretations of the Aristotelian Enthymene." *PMASAL*, 21(1936):489–500.

7   McKEON, Richard. "Aristotle's Conception of Language and the Arts of Language." *C&C*, pp. 176–231.

8   McMAHON, A. P. "On the Second Book of Aristotle's *Poetics* and the Source of Theophrastus' Definition of Tragedy." *HSCP*, 28(1917):1–46.*

9   ——. "Seven Questions on Aristotelian Definitions of Tragedy and Comedy." *HSCP*, 40(1929):97–198.

10 MARGOLIOUTH, David Samuel. *The Poetics of Aristotle Translated from Greek into English and from Arabic into Latin*. London, 1911.

11 MARSA, E. "Ruggero Bacone e la Poetica di Aristotele." *GCFI*, 32(1953): 457–73.

12 MARSH, Robert. "Aristotle and the Modern Rhapsode." *QJS*, 39(1953): 481–89.

13 MARSHALL, John S. "Art and Aesthetic in Aristotle." *JAAC*, 12:228–31.

14 O'CONNOR, William Van. "Aristotle and Modern Criticism." *CEA*, 24(1962):1, 4–5.

15 OLSON, Elder, ed. *Aristotle's Poetics and English Literature: A Collection of Critical Essays*. Chicago: U of Chicago P, 1965. Phoenix. PhC7]*†

16 OSTWALD, Martin. "Aristotle on Harmatia and Sophocles' Oedipus Tyrannus." In *Festschrift Ernst Kapp*, Hamburg: von Schröder, 1958. Pp. 93–108.

17 PITCHER, Seymour M. "Aristotle on Poetic Art." *JGE*, 7(1952):56–76.

18 ——. "Aristotle's Good and Just Heroes." *PQ*, 24(1945):1–11:190–91.

19 POST, Levi Arnold. "Aristotle and the Philosophy of Fiction." In his *From Homer to Meander*. Berkeley: U of California P, 1951. Pp. 245–69.

20 RANSOM, John Crowe. "The Cathartic Principle." See 6.7

21 ROSS, William David. *Aristotle*. London: Methuen, 1930. UP-65. B&N]

22 ROSTAGNI, Augusto. See 9.6.*

23 SKULSKY, Harold. "Aristotle's *Poetics* Revisited." *JHI*, 19(1958), 147–60.

24 SOLMSEN, F. "The Origins and Methods of Aristotle's *Poetics*." *Classical Quarterly*, 29(1935), 192–201.

25 TRACY, H. "Aristotle on Aesthetic Pleasure." *Classical Philology*, 41:43–6.

26 VAHLEN, Johann. *Beiträge zu Aristoteles Poetik*, ed. Hermann Schöne. Leipzig, 1914.

27 WEINBERG, Bernard. "From Aristotle to Pseudo-Aristotle." *CL*, 5:97–104.

1 WIMSATT, William K. "Aristotle and Oedipus or Else." In his *Hateful Contraries: Studies in Literature and Criticism*. Lexington: U of Kentucky P, 1965.

St. Augustine

2 [Aurelius Augustinus, Bishop of Hippo.] *De doctrina christiana libri quattuor*, ed. G. M. Green. Vienna: Hoelder-Pichler-Tempsky, 1963. [C.S.E. 80] [For literary criticism see especially Book IV.]

3 *On Christian Doctrine*, trans. D. W. Robertson, Jr. Indianapolis: Bobbs-Merrill, 1958. [LLA, 80.] [For literary criticism see especially Book IV.]

*   *   *

4 CHAPMAN, Emmanuel. *Saint Augustine's Philosophy of Beauty*. London: Sheed and Ward, 1939.

5 ———. "Some Aspects of St. Augustine's Philosophy of Beauty." *JAAC* 1(1941):46–51.

6 HENRY, Paul. See 17.14.

7 KNIGHT, W. F. Jackson. *"De Musica": A Synopsis*. London: Ontological Institute, 1949.

8 MAZZEO, Joseph Anthony. "The Augustian Conception of Beauty and Dante's *Convivio*." *JAAC*, 15(1957):435–48.*

9 SVOBODA, Karel. *L'Esthétique de St. Augustine et ses sources*. Brno: Press of the Philosophical Faculty of Masaryk University, 1933.

Cicero

10 [Marcus Tullius Cicero.] *Ad C. Herrennium de ratione dicendi* (*Rhetorica ad herennium*), trans. Harry Caplan. Cambridge, mass.: Harvard U P, 1964. [Loeb ed.]

11 *Brutus*, trans. G. L. Hendrickson: *Orator*, trans. H. M. Hubbell. Rev. and repr. ed. Cambridge, Mass.: Harvard U P, 1962. Latin and English.]

12 *De inventione, De optimo genere, Oratum topica*, trans. H. M. Hubbell. Cambridge, Mass.: Harvard U P, 1960. Loeb ed.] For literary criticism see especially *De inventione*.]

13 *De oratore*, trans. E. W. Sutton and H. Rackham. 2 vols. Rev. ed. Cambridge, Mass.: Harvard U P, 1959–60. [Loeb ed.]

14 *Epistulae*, eds. Ludovicus Claude Purser, W. S. Watt and D. R. S. Bailey. 3 vols. Oxford: Clarendon P, 1957–65. [Oxford Classical Tests.] [For literary criticism see especially "Epistula ad L. Lucceium."]

15 *Letters*, ed. and trans. L. P. Wilkinson. London: Hutchinson, 1966. [For literary criticism see especially "Letter to Lucius Lucceius."] [Norton N454]†

16 *The Speeches*, trans. N. H. Watts. Cambridge, Mass.: Harvard U P, 1961. Loeb ed.] For literary criticism see especially "Pro Archia."]

*   *   *

17 FISKE, George Converse, and Mary A. GRANT. See. 8.9.

18 GUILLEMAN, A. "Cicéron et la culture latine." *REL*, 25(1947):148–57.

19 SCOTT, Izora. See 27.1.

Demetrius

1 [Demetrius of Phaleron.] *A Greek Critic: Demetrius on Style*, ed. and trans. G. M. A. Grube. Toronto: U of Toronto P, 1961.

2 *On Style*. See 1.15.

Dionysius of Halicarnassus

3 *Dionysius of Halicarnassus on Literary Composition*, ed. and trans. W. R. Roberts. London: Macmillan, 1910. [Greek and English.]

4 *The Three Literary Letters*, ed. and trans. W. Rhys Roberts. Cambridge: U P, 1901. [Latin and English.]

Fronto

5 [Marcus Cornelius Fronto.] *The Correspondence of Marcus Cornelius Fronto with Marcus Aurelius Antoninus, Lucius Verus, Antoninus Pius, and Various Friends*, ed. and trans. C. R. Haines. 2 vols. New York: Putnam, 1919–20. [Loeb ed.] [For literary criticism see especially "De eloquentia liber," "De orationibus."]

6 *M. Cornelii Frontonis Epistulae*, ed. M. P. J. Van Den Hout. Leiden: Brill, 1954.

Aulus Gellius

7 *The Attic Nights of Aulus Gellius*, trans. John C. Rolph. 3 vols. New York: Putnam, 1927–28. [Loeb ed.] [For literary criticism see especially paragraphs dealing with style, vocabulary, and translations.]

Heracleitus

8 *Allégories d'Homère*, ed. and trans. Felix Buffière. Paris: Belles Lettres, 1962. [French and Greek].

9 *Heracliti Quaestiones Homericae*, ed. Societatis Philologa Bouensis. Leipzig: Teubner, 1910.

Horace

10 [Quintus Horatius Flaccus.] *Arte poetica di Orazio*, ed. Augusto Rostagni. Torino: Chiantore, 1930. [Library of Classical Philology, directed by G. De Sanctis and A. Rostagni.]*

11 "Epistle to the Pisos," trans. J. H. and S. C. Smith. *GC*, pp. 114–28.

12 *Horace on Poetry*, trans. Charles Oscar Brink. Cambridge: U P, 1963.

14

1 *Horace on the Art of Poetry*, trans. E. H. Blakeney. London: Scholartis, 1928.

2 *Satires, Epistles, Ars Poetica*, trans. H. R. Fairclough. Cambridge, Mass.: Harvard U P, 1961. [Loeb ed.] [For literary criticism see especially *Ars Poetica*, "Epistle to Pisos."]

*   *   *

3 ANDERSON, W. S. "'Poetic Fiction'—Horace, *Serm.* 1.5." *CW*, IL 49(1955–56):57–9.

4 ARDIZZONI, A. "Il Problema della satira in Orazio." *RFC*, 27(1949): 161–76.

5 BRINK, Charles Oscar. *Horace on Poetry*. Cambridge: U P, 1963.

6 CAMPBELL, Archibald Young. *Horace: A New Interpretation*. London: Methuen, 1924.

7 COMMAGER, Steele. "Literary Conventions and Stylistic Criticism in the Augustan Age." In his *The Odes of Horace: A Critical Study*. New Haven: Yale U P, 1962.

8 COOK, Albert S. See 1.7.

9 D'ALTON, John Francis. *Horace and His Age*. London and New York: Longmans, Green, 1917.

10 D'ANTÒ, V. "Ancora sulla critica di Orazio a Lucilio." *MCl*, XVIII (1951):10–17.

11 FAIRCLOUGH, Henry Rushton. "Horace's View of the Relations Between Satire and Comedy." *AJP*, 34(1913):183–93.

12 FISKE, George Converse. See 8.8.*

13 ———, and Mary A. GRANT. See 8.9.

14 FRANK, Tenney. "Horace's Definition of Poetry." *CJ*, 31(1935):167–74.

15 GRIMAL, Pierre. *Horace: Art Poétique; Commentaire et Étude*. Paris Centre de Documentation Universitaire, 1964.

16 HENDRICKSON, George Lincoln. "Horace, *Serm.* I, 4: A Protest and a Programme." *AJP*, 21(1900):121–42.

17 IMMISCH, Otto. *Horazens Epistel über die Dichtkunst*. Leipzig, 1932. [*Philologus* (Supplement 24, No. 3).]

18 LA DRIÈRE, Craig. "Horace and the Theory of Imitation." *AJP*, 60:288–300.

19 OTIS, Brooks. "Horace and the Elegists." *TAPA*, 76(1945), 177–90.

20 SAINTONGE, Paul F., et al. *Horace: Three Phases of His Influence: Lectures Given at Mount Holyoke College*. Chicago: U of Chicago P, 1936.

21 SELLAR, Willian Young. *The Roman Poets of the Augustan Ages Horace and the Elegaic Poets*. New York: Bilbo and Tannen, 1965. [Reprint of 1st ed. published in 1892.]

22 SHOWERMAN, Grant. *Horace and His Influence*. Boston: Marshall Jones, 1922.

23 STEIDLE, Wolf. *Studien zur Ars Poetica des Horaz*. Würzburg-Aumühle: Triltsch, 1939.

24 WILKINSON, L. P. *Horace and His Lyric Poetry*. Cambridge: U P, 1945. [Gordian. 553]†

Longinus

25 [Cassius Longinus.] See 1.15.

26 *Del Sublime*, ed. and trans. Augusto Rostagni. Milan: I.E.I., 1947.

1   *Longinus on the Sublime*, trans. William R. Roberts. Cambridge: U P, 1935.

2   "Longinus on the Sublime." *GC*, pp. 65–111.

3   *"Longinus" on the Sublime*, ed. D. A. Russell. Oxford: Clarendon P, 1964.

4   *On Elevation of Style*, trans. T. G. Tucker. London: Oxford U P, 1935.

5   *On Great Writing (On the Sublime)*, trans. G. M. A. Grube. Indianapolis: Bobbs-Merrill, 1957. [LLA, 79.]†

6   "On Literary Excellence," trans. A. H. Gilbert. *LC*, pp. 146–98.

*   *   *

7   BOYD, M. J. "Longinus, the 'Philological Discourses' and the Essay 'On the Sublime.'" *Classical Quarterly*, n.s. 7 (1959): 39–46.

8   BRODY, Jules. See 65.9.

9   GODOLPHIN, F. R. B. "The Basic Critical Doctrine of Longinus' *On the Sublime*." *Transactions and Proceedings of the American Philological Association*, 68(1937): 172–83.

10 GRUBE, Georges Maximilien Antoine. "Notes on the Peri Hupsous." *AJP*, 78(1957): 355–74.

11 HENN, Thomas Rice. See 5.4.

12 MENUEZ, C. F. "Longinus on the Equivalence of the Arts." *CJ*, 36:346–53.

13 MONK, Samuel Holt. *The Sublime*. See 57.17.*

14 OLSON, Elder. "The Argument of Longinus' *On the Sublime*." *MP*, 39 (1942): 225–58.

15 SEGAL, Charles P. "Hupsous and the Problem of Cultural Decline in the *De Sublimitate*." *Harvard Studies in Classical Philology*, 64 (1959): 121–46.

16 TATE, Allen. See 6.17.

Macrobius

17 [Ambrosius Aurelius Theodosius Macrobius.] *Commentary on the Dream of Scipio*, trans. W. H. Stahl. New York: Columbia U P, 1952.

18 *Les Saturnales*, trans. Henri Borneque and François Richard. 2 vols. Paris: Garnier, 1937. [Latin and French.]

19 *Saturnalia*. 2 vols. Leipzig: Teubner, 1963.

20 *Saturnalia*, trans. Percival V. Davies. New York: Columbia U P, 1968. [Records of Civilization Series.]

*   *   *

21 HENRY, Paul. See 17.14.

Philo Judaeus

22 *Philo*, trans. F. H. Colson and G. H. Whitaker. 10 vols. Cambridge, Mass.: Harvard U P, 1958–62. [Loeb ed.]

23 *Philo*. Supplement I. *Questions and Answers on Genesis*, trans. Ralph Marcus. Cambridge, Mass.: Harvard U P, 1953. [Loeb ed.]

24 *Philo*. Supplement II. *Questions and Answers on Exodus*, trans. Ralph Marcus. Cambridge, Mass.: Harvard U P, 1953. [Loeb ed.]

Plato

1 *Dialogues*, trans. Benjamin Jowett. New York: Macmillan, 1892.

2 *Dialogues of Plato: Apology, Crito, Phaedo, Symposium, Republic*, trans. Benjamin Jowett, ed. J. D. Kaplan. New York: Pocket, 1955. WSP-W207]†

3 *The Laws of Plato*, trans. A. E. Taylor. London: Dent, 1934.

4 *Plato*, trans. Harold North Fowler and others. 10 vols. Cambridge, Mass.: Harvard U P, 1952–60. [Loeb ed.]

5 *Plato: On the Trial and Death of Socrates. Euthyphro, Apology, Crito, Phaedo*, trans. Lane Cooper. Ithaca: Cornell U P, 1941.

6 *Plato: Phaedrus, Ion, Gorgias, and Symposium, with Passages from the Republic and Laws*, trans. Lane Cooper. London: Oxford U P, 1938.

7 *Plato's Phaedrus*, trans. Reginald Hackforth. Cambridge: U P, 1952. [LLA 119]†

8 "The Republic." *LC*, pp. 24–55. [Selections.]

*   *   *

9 AGAR, Herbert. See 3.2.

10 ANDERSON, A. H. "Notes on Plato's Aesthetic." *PhR*, 48:65–70.

11 BRÉMOND, Henri. "Platon et la poésie exilée." In his *Prière et poésie*. Paris: Grasset, 1926.

12 CAVARNOS, Constantine. "Plato's Teaching on Fine Art." *PPR*, 13:487–98.

13 COLLINGWOOD, Robin George. *The Principles of Art*. Oxford: Clarendon P, 1938.

14 DeLACY, Phillip. "Plato and the Method of the Arts." In *The Classical Tradition: Literary and Historical Studies in Honor of Harry Caplan*, ed. Luitpold Wallach. Ithaca: Cornell U P, 1966, pp. 123–32.

15 DUNCAN, P. "The Place of Art in Plato's Ideal State." *UTQ*, 10:27–38.

16 FINSLER, Georg August. *Platon und die aristotelische Poetik*. Leipzig: Spirgatis, 1900.*

17 GILBERT, Allan H. "Did Plato Banish the Poets or the Critics?" *SP*, 36(1939):1–19.

18 GILBERT, Katharine E. "The Relation of the Moral to the Aesthetic Standard in Plato." *PhR*, 43(1934):279–94.

19 GREENE, William Chase. "Plato's View of Poetry." *HSCP*, 29(1918):1–75.

20 GRUBE, Georges Maximilien Antoine. *Plato's Thought*. London: Methuen, 1935. [Beacon-BP60]*†

21 LA DRIÈRE, Craig. "The Problem of Plato's *Ion*." *JAAC*, 10(1951):26–34.

1 LODGE, Rupert Clendon. *Plato's Theory of Art.* London: Routledge and Kegan Paul, 1963.

2 PANOFSKY, Erwin. *Idea: Ein Beitrag zur Begriffsgeschichte der älteren Kunsttheorie.* Leipzig: Teubner, 1924.* [*Idea: A Concept in Art Theory,* trans. J. S. Peake. Columbia: U of South Carolina P, 1968.]

3 REDFIELD, James. "A Lecture on Plato's *Apology.*" *JGE,* 15:93–108.

4 SCHUHL, Pierre-Maxime. *Platon et l'art de son temps.* Paris: Alcan, 1933.

5 SHOREY, Paul. *What Plato Said.* Chicago: U of Chicago P, 1933. [Phoenix-P184]*†

6 TAYLOR, A. E. *Plato.* London: Constable, 1908.

7 VERDENIUS, Willem Jacob. *Mimesis: Plato's Doctrine of Artistic Imitation and Its Meaning to Us.* Leiden: Brill, 1949.

8 VICAIRE, Paul. *Platon critique littéraire.* Paris: Klincksieck, 1960.

Plotinus

9 *Ennéades,* ed. and trans. Émile Bréhier. 7 vols. Paris, 1924–54. [Collection des Universités de France.]

10 *Ennéades,* trans. Stephen McKenna. 2d ed. rev. London: Faber and Faber, 1956.

11 *Plotinus,* ed. and trans. A. H. Armstrong. Cambridge, Mass.: Harvard U P, 1966–67. [Loeb ed.]

12 DODDS, E. R., ed. and trans., *Select Passages* . . . . See 1.9.

* * *

13 CLARK, Gordon H. "φαντασία in Plotinus." *Philosophical Essays in Honor of Edward Arthur Singer, Jr.,* eds. F. P. Clark and M. C. Nahm. Philadelphia: U of Pennsylvania P, 1942, pp. 297–309.

14 ———. "Plotinus' Theory of Sensation." *PhR,* 51:357–82.

15 HENRY, Paul. *Plotin et l'Occident: Firmicus Maternus, Marius Victorinus, St. Augustine et Macrobe.* Louvaine: Spicilegium Sacrum Lovaniense, 1934. [Repr. Dubuque, Iowa, 1967.]

16 KEYSER, Eugenie de. *La Signification de l'art dans les Ennéades de Plotin.* Louvain: U de Louvain, 1955. [Recueil de travaux d'histoire et de philologie.]

17 KOCH, Franz. *Goethe und Plotin.* Leipzig, 1925.

18 VANNI, Bourbon di Petrella, Fiammetta. *Il Problema dell'arte e della bellezza in Plotino.* Florence: Le Monnier, 1956.

Plutarch

19 "The Life of St. Basil and the Address to Young Men." In Padelford, F. M,. see 6.1.

1   *Moralia*, ed. and trans. F. C. Babbitt. 14 vols. New York: Putnam, 1927–67. [Loeb ed.] [For literary criticism see especially "How a Young Man Should Read the Poets" and "On Isis and Osiris."]

Porphyry

2   Porphyry the Philosopher.] *On the Cave of Nymphs in the Thirteenth Book of the Odyssey*, trans. Thomas Taylor. London: Watkins, 1917.

3   *Philosophi Platonici Opuscula*, ed. Augustus Nauck. Hildesheim: Olms, 1963. [For literary criticism see especially *De Antro Nympharum*.]

*   *   *

4   DÖRRIE, Heinrich, ed. *Porphyre: 8 exposés suivis de discussions.* Geneva: Foundation Hardt, 1966.

Proclus

5   [Proclus Diadochus.] *Procli Diadochi in Platonis Rempublicam commentarii*, ed. G. Kroll. 2 vols. Leipzig: Teubner, 1899–1901.

*   *   *

6   FRIEDL, Ansgar Josef. *Die Homer-Interpretation des Proklos.* Dresden, 1936.

7   ROSÁN, Laurence. *The Philosophy of Proclus: The Final Phase of Ancient Thought.* New York: Cosmos, 1949.

Quintilian

8   [Marcus Fabius Quintilianus.] *The Institutio Oratoria of Quintilian*, trans. H. E. Butler. Cambridge, Mass.: Harvard U P, 1958. [Loeb ed.] [For literary criticism see especially Book X.]

*   *   *

9   BRANDENBURG, Ernest. "Quintilian and the Good Orator." *QJS*, 34(1948):23–29.

Seneca

10   [Marcus Annaeus Seneca.] *The Suasoriae of Seneca the Elder*, ed. and trans. William A. Edward. Cambridge: U P, 1928. [Latin and English.]

*   *   *

11   BARDON, H. *Le Vocabulaire de la critique littéraire chez Sénèque le rhéteur.* Paris: Les Belles Lettres, 1940.

12   SOCHATOFF, A. F. "The Basic Rhetorical Theories of the Elder Seneca." *CJ*, 34(1938–39):345–54.

Tacitus

13   [Cornelius Tacitus.] *The Complete Works of Tacitus*, trans. Alfred John Church and William Jackson Brodribb, ed. Moses Hadas. New York: Modern Library, 1942. [For literary criticism see especially "A Dialogue on Oratory."] [Modern Library-T53.]

14   *Dialogus, Agricola, Germania*, trans. William Peterson and Maurice Hutton. Cambridge, Mass.: Harvard U P, 1958. [Loeb ed.] [For literary criticism see especially *Dialogus de oratoribus*.]

1 *Libri qui supersunt*, post C. Halm, G. Andresen octavum edidit-Ericus Koes termann. 2 vols. Leipzig: Teubner, 1957–61. [Teubner Library of Greek and Roman writings.]

2 *The Works of Tacitus*, Oxford trans., rev. New York: Harper, 1858.

Tertullian

3 [Quintus Septimus Florens Tertullianus.] *Tertullian: Apology and De Spectaculis with an English Translation*, ed. and trans. T. R. Glover. Putnam, 1931. [Loeb ed.]

Theophrastus

4 *Characters*, ed. and trans. J. M. Edmonds. Cambridge, Mass.: Harvard U P, 1961. [Loeb ed.]

* * *

5 GORDON, George Stuart. "Theophrastus and His Imitators." In *English Literature and the Classics*, ed. G. S. Gordon. Oxford: Clarendon P, 1912, pp. 49–86.

6 McMAHON, A. P. See 11.8.*

Medieval Criticism

General

7 ABELSON, Paul. *The Seven Liberal Arts: A Study in Mediaeval Culture*. New York: Russell and Russell, 1965. [Teachers College Contributions to Education, 11.]

8 ARBUSOW, Leonid. *Colores Retorici*. Göttingen: Vandenhoeck and Ruprecht, 1963.

9 ATKINS, John William Hey. See 3.4.

10 BALDWIN, Charles Sears. *Medieval Rhetoric and Poetic (to 1400), Interpreted from Representative Works*. Gloucester, Mass.: Smith, 1959.

11 BARRETT, Cyril. "Medieval Art Criticism." *BJA*, 5(1965):25–36.

12 BETHURUM, Dorothy. *Critical Approaches to Medieval Literature*. New York: Columbia U P, 1961.

13 BRINKMANN, Hennig. *Zu Wesen und Form mittelalterlicher Dichtung*. Halle: Niemeyer, 1928.

14 BRUYNE, Edgar de. *Études d'esthétique médiévale*. 3 vols. Brussels: De Tempel, 1946.*

1 CURTIUS, Ernst Robert. *Europäishe Literature und lateinisches Mittelalter.* Bern: Francke, 1948. [*European Literature and the Latin Middle Ages*, trans. Willard Trask. London: Routledge and Kegan Paul, 1953.]

2 DAVLIN, Sister May Clemente, O. P. "*Treuthe* in *Piers Plowman:* A Study in Style and Sensibility." *DA*, 25:1905 (Calif).

3 DUNBAR, Helen Flanders. *Symbolism in Medieval Thought.* New York: Russell and Russell, 1961.

4 FARAL, Edmond. *Les Arts poétiques du XIIième et du XIIIième siècle: Recherches et documents sur la technique littéraire du moyen âge.* Paris: Champion, 1924.*

5 GLUNZ, H. H. *Die Literaturästhetik des Europäischen Mittelalters.* Frankfurt: Klostermann, 1963.

6 HALM, Karl von. See 1.18.

7 HANSON, Richard Patrick Crossland. *Allegory and Event: A Study of the Sources and Significance of Origen's Interpretation of Scripture.* London: SCM Press, 1959.

8 JOHNSTONE, Grahame. "Medieval Criticism: A Comment." *MCR*, 4:127–32.

9 KELLY, Douglas. "The Scope of the Treatment of Composition in the Twelfth- and Thirteenth-Century Arts of Poetry." *Speculum*, 41(1966):261–78.

10 LOBEL, Edgar. "The Medieval Latin Poetics." *PBA*, 17(1931):309–34.

11 LUBAC, Henri de. *Exégèse médiévale.* 2 vols. Paris: Aubier, 1959.

12 McKEON, Richard. "Poetry and Philosophy in the Twelfth Century: The Renaissance of Rhetoric." *C&C*, pp. 297–318.

13 ———. "Rhetoric in the Middle Ages." *C&C*, pp. 260–96.

14 MANDONNET, Pierre Felix. *Siger de Brabant et l'averroïsme latin.* 2 vols in 1. 2d ed. rev. and enl. Louvain, 1911.

15 MONTANO, Rocco. *L'Estetica nel pensiero cristiano.* Milan, 1955.

16 ONG, Walter J. "Wit and Mystery: A Revaluation in Mediaeval Latin Hymnody." *Speculum*, 22(1947):310–41.

17 PARÉ, Gerard Marie, Adrien BRUNET, and Pierre TREMBLAY. *La Renaissance du XIIième siècle: Les écoles et l'enseignement.* Paris: Vrin, 1933.

18 QUADLBAUER, Franz. *Die antike Theorien der genera dicendi in Lateinischen Mittelalter.* Vienna: H. Böhlauf, 1962. [*SÖAW*, 191: 2]

19 RENAN, Ernest. *Averroes et l'averroïsme: Essai historique.* 4th ed. rev. and enl. Paris, 1852.

20 RICHARDSON, Lilla Janette. "Irony Through Imagery: A Chaucerian Technique Studied in Relation to Sources, Analogues, and the Dicta of Medieval Rhetoric." *DA*, 24:1176–77 (Calif).

1 ROBINS, H. *Ancient and Medieval Grammatical Theory.* London, 1951.

2 ROOS, Heinrich. *Die Modi Significandi des Martinus de Dacea.* Münster: Westfalen, 1952.

3 SANDKÜHLER, Bruno. *Die frühen Dantekommentare und ihr Verhältnis zur mittelalterlichen Kommentartradition.* Munich: Hueber, 1967.

4 SAULNIER, Verdun L. *La Littérature française du Moyen Age.* 6th ed. rev- Paris: P U de France, 1964.

5 SPEARING, A. C. *Criticism and Medieval Poetry.* London: Arnold, 1964.

6 SPENGEL, Leonhard von. *Rhetores Graeci.* 3 vols. Leipzig: Teubner, 1854–85.

Individual Authors

Alcuin

7 "Disputatio de Rhetorica." See Halm, Karl von, 1.18.

8 *The Rhetoric of Alcuin and Charlemagne,* ed. and trans. Wilbur Samuel Howell. New York: Russell and Russell, 1965. [Latin and English.]

St. Thomas Aquinas

9 CALLAHAN, Leonard. *A Theory of Esthetic, According to the Principles of St. Thomas Aquinas.* Washington, D.C.: Catholic U, 1927.

10 COOMARASWAMY, A. K. "Medieval Aesthetic II: St. Thomas Aquinas on Dionysius and a Note on the Relation of Beauty to Truth." *Art Bulletin,* 20:66–77.

11 DUFFY, John A. *A Philosophy of Poetry Based on Thomistic Principles.* Washington, D.C., The Catholic University of America 1945.

12 GILSON, Étienne. *The Philosophy of St. Thomas Aquinas,* trans. Edward Bullough, ed. G. A. Elrington. 2d ed. rev. St. Louis: Herder, 1939.*

13 STEINBERG, C. S. "The Aesthetic Theory of St. Thomas Aquinas." *PhR,* 50:483–97.

Averroes

14 [Averroes-Hermannus Alemannus.] *Averrois Cordubensis Commentarium Medium in Aristotelis Poetarium,* ed. William F. Goggess. Dissertation, U of North Carolina, 1965.

*   *   *

15 MARGOLIOUTH, David Samuel. See 11.10.

16 MARSA, E. See 11.11.

17 RENAN, Ernest. See 20.19.

St. Basil the Great

1   "On the Right Use of Greek Poetry." See 6.1.

*   *   *

2   PLUTARCH. "The Life of St. Basil and the Address to Young Men." See 17.19.

St. Bede

3   [The Venerable Bede.] *De Arte Metrica*. Vol. VII of *Grammatici Latini*, ed. Heinrich Keil. 7 vols. Leipzig: Teubner, 1897–1923.

4   "De Orthographia." See Halm, Karl von, 1.18.

5   "De Schematibus et Tropis." See Halm, Karl von, 1.18.

St. Bonaventure

6   GILSON, Étienne. *The Philosophy of St. Bonaventure*. New York: Sheed and Ward, 1938.*

Cassiodorus

7   [Flavius Magnus Aurelius Cassiodorus.] *An Introduction to Divine and Human Readings*, trans. Leslie W. Jones. New York: Columbia U P, 1946.

8   *Opera*, ed. M. Adriaen. Turnhout, Belgium: Brepols, 1958–

Geoffrey Chaucer

9   MANLY, J. M. "Chaucer and the Rhetoricians." *PBA*, 22(1926):95–113.*

10   RENOIR, Alain. "Tradition and Moral Realism: Chaucer's Conception of the Poet." *SN*, 35(1963):199–210.

11   SIMMONS, J. L. "The Place of the Poet in Chaucer's House of Fame." *MLQ*, 27(1966): 125–35.

12   WOODBRIDGE, Elisabeth. "Chaucer's Classicism." *JEGP*, 1(1897):111–17.

Dante

13   [Dante Alighieri.] *Il Convivio*, ed. Antonio Enzo Quaglio. 2d ed. Florence: Le Monnier, 1964.

1 *La Correspondenza poetica di Dante Alighieri e Giovanni del Virgilio*, eds. E. Bolgiani and M. Valglimigli. Florence: Olschki, 1964. [Latin and Italian.]

2 *Dante's Convivio*, trans. William Walrond Jackson. Oxford: Clarendon P, 1909.

3 *Dante's Treatise "De Vulgari Eloquentia,"* trans. A. G. F. Howell. London: Paul, Trench, Trübner, 1890.

4 *Dantis Aligherii Epistolae: The Letters of Dante*, ed. and trans. Paget Toynbee. 2d ed. Oxford: Clarendon P, 1966. [Latin and English.]

5 "Letter to Can Grande Della Scala." *LC*, pp. 202–6. [In part.]

6 *The New Life: La Vita Nuova*, trans. William Anderson. Baltimore: Penguin, 1964. [L130]†

7 *A Translation of the Latin Works of Dante Alighieri*, trans. A. G. F. Howell and Philip H. Wicksteed. London: Dent, 1904.

8 *Tutte le opere di Dante*, ed. Fredi Chiapelli. Milan: Mursia, 1965.

* * *

9 EWERT, Alfred. "Dante's Theory of Diction." *Modern Humanities Research Association*, No. 31 (1959): 15–30.

10 GARDNER, Edmund Garratt. "Dante as a Literary Critic." In *Dante: Essays in Commemoration, 1321–1921*, ed. Antonio Cippico. London: U of London P, 1921, pp. 81–104.

11 HATZFELD, Helmut. "Modern Literary Scholarship as Reflected in Dante Criticism." *CL*, 3(1951):289–309.

12 MARIGO, Aristede. *De vulgari eloquentia: Ridotto a miglior lezione*, trans. and commentary A. Marigo. Florence: Monnier, 1948. [*Opera di Dante*. New ed. Vol. VI.]

13 MAZZEO, Joseph Anthony. See 12.8.*

14 SINGLETON, Charles S. "Dante's Allegory." *Speculum*, 25(1950):78–86.

15 VITTORINI, Domenico. "Dante's Contribution in Esthetics." *Italica*, 23(1946):265–74.*

Gervais de Melcheley

16 [Gervasius of Melcheley.] *Ars Poetica*, ed. Hans-Jurgen Grabener. Münster, n.p. 1965. [Forschungen zur Romanischen Philologie, 17.]

Henry d'Andeli

17 [13th century.] *The Battle of the Seven Arts: A French Poem*, ed. and trans. A. J. Paeton. Berkeley: U of California P, 1914.

St. Isidore of Seville

18 [Isidorus, Bishop of Seville.] *Etymologiarum sive Originum Libri XX*, ed. W. M. Lindsay. 2 vols. Oxford: Clarendon P., 1911.

Richard de Bury

1 [Richard Aungerville, Bishop of Durham.] *The Love of Books: The Philobiblon of Richard de Bury*, ed. and trans. E. C. Thomas. New York: Cooper Square, 1966.

William of Moerbake

2 [Gulielmus de Morbeka, Archbishop of Corinth.] *Aristotelis de Arte Poetica*, ed. E. Valgimigli. Paris, 1953.

Renaissance Criticism

General

3 ATKINS, John William Hey. See 3.4.

4 BALDWIN, Charles Sears. *Renaissance Literary Theory and Practice: Classicism in the Rhetoric and Poetic of Italy, France and England, 1400–1600*, ed. Donald Lemen Clark. Gloucester, Mass.: Smith, 1959.

5 BETHELL, Samuel Leslie. "The Two Universes in Literary Theory and Practice." In his *The Cultural Revolution of the Seventeenth Century*. London: Dobson, 1963.

6 BLUNT, Anthony. *Artistic Theory in Italy (1450–1600)*. Oxford: Clarendon P, 1940. [50]*

7 BONORA, Ettore. *Sulla critica e l'estetica de Cinquecento.* Torino: Gheroni, 1963.

8 BORINSKI, Karl. *Die Poetik der Renaissance.* Berlin: Weidmann, 1886.

9 BUCK, August. *Italienische Dichtungslehren vom Mittelalter bis zum Ausgang der Renaissance.* Tübingen: Niemeyer, 1952.

10 BULLOCK, W. L. "Italian Sixteenth Century Criticism." *MLN*, 41(1926): 254–63.

11 BUNDY, Murray W. "Invention and Imagination in the Renaissance." *JEGP*, 29:535–45.

12 BUSH, Douglas. "The Classics and Imaginative Literature." In his *Prefaces to Renaissance Literature*. Cambridge, Mass.: Harvard U P, 1965. [Lectures.] [Norton. N187]†

13 ——. *Mythology and the Renaissance Tradition in English Poetry.* London: Milford, Oxford U P, 1932.*

14 BUXTON, John. *Elizabethan Taste.* London: Macmillan, 1963.

15 CARR, C. T. "Two Words in Art History: I. Baroque; II. Rococo." *FMLS*, 1:175–90;266–81.

1   CASTOR, Grahame. *Pléiade Poetics: A Study in Sixteenth-Century Thought and Terminology.* Cambridge: U P, 1964.

2   CLARK, Donald Lemen. *Rhetoric and Poetry in the Renaissance: A Study of Rhetorical Terms in English Renaissance Literary Criticism.* New York: Russell and Russell, 1963. [Columbia University Studies in English and Comparative Literature.]

3   CLEMENTS, Robert John. *Critical Theory and Practice of the Pléiade.* Cambridge, Mass.: Harvard U P, 1942.*

4   ———. *Picta poesis: Literary and Humanistic Theory in Renaissance Emblem Books.* Rome: Storia e Letteratura, 1960.

5   CRANE, William Garrett. *Wit and Rhetoric in the Renaissance.* New York: Columbia U P, 1937.

6   CROCE, Benedetto. *Storia dell'età Barocca in Italia: Pensiero-poesia e letterature-vita morale.* 2d ed. rev. Bari: Laterza, 1946.*

7   DAVIDSON, Hugh M. *Audience, Words and Art: Studies in Seventeenth-Century French Rhetoric.* Columbus: Ohio State U P, 1965.

8   DEANE, C. V. *Dramatic Theory and the Rhymed Heroic Play.* London: Milford, Oxford U P, 1931.

9   DORAN, Madeline. *Endeavors of Art: A Study of Form in Elizabethan Drama.* Madison: U of Wisconsin P, 1954. [U of Wisconsin P-W37]†

10 ELLEDGE, Scott, and Donald SCHIER. See 1.13.

11 ENRIGHT, Dennis, and Ernst DE CHICHERA. See 1.14.

12 GEBERT, Clara. See 1.16.

13 GIOVANNINI, G. "Historical Realism and the Tragic Emotions in Renaissance Criticism." *PQ*, 32(1953):304–20.

14 GIRALDI, Giovanni. *L'Estetica italiana nella prima metà del secolo XV: Figure e problemi.* Pisa: Lischi, 1963.

15 GRAY, Hanna H. "Renaissance Humanism: The Pursuit of Eloquence." *JHI*, 24:497–514.

16 HALL, Robert A., Jr. *The Italian Questione della Lingua: An Interpretive Essay.* Chapel Hill: U of North Carolina P, 1942. [UNCSRLL, 4]

17 HALL, Vernon. *Renaissance Literary Criticism: A Study of Its Social Content.* New York: Columbia U P, 1945. [Reprint Gloucester, Mass.: Smith, 1959.]*

18 HARDISON, Osborne Bennett, Jr. *The Enduring Monument: A Study of the Idea of Praise in Renaissance Literary Theory and Practice.* Chapel Hill: U of North Carolina P, 1962.*

19 ———. See 1.19.

20 HASLEWOOD, Joseph. See 2.1.

21 HATHAWAY, Baxter. *The Age of Criticism: The Late Renaissance in Italy.* Ithaca: Corness U P, 1962.*

22 ———. *Marvels and Commonplaces: Renaissance Literary Criticism.* New York: Random House, 1968. [X520.]†

26   RENAISSANCE CRITICISM

1   HATZFELD, Helmut A. "Baroque Style: Ideology and the Arts." *BuR*, 7(1957):71–9.

2   HERRICK, Marvin T. *Comic Theory in the Sixteenth Century.* Urbana: U of Illinois P, 1964. [1950.]

3   ———. See 8.17.

4   ———. *Italian Comedy in the Renaissance.* Urbana: U of Illinois P, 1966.

5   ———. *Italian Tragedy in the Renaissance.* Urbana: U of Illinois P. 1965.

6   HOWELL, Wilbur Samuel. *Logic and Rhetoric in England, 1500–1700.* Princeton: Princeton U P, 1956.

7   HUDSON, Herman Cleophus. "The Development of Dramatic Criticism in England and Spain During the Elizabethan Period and the Golden Age." *DA*, 23(1962):235 (Mich).

8   JOSEPH, Bertram L. "Character and Plot: Towards Standards of Criticism for Elizabethan Drama." *DramS*, 3:541–44.

9   ———. " 'Scenes Invented Merely to be Spoken': Towards Standards of Criticism for Elizabethan Drama." *DramS*, 1:18–33.

10 KERNODLE, George Riley. *From Art to Theatre: Form and Convention in the Renaissance.* Chicago: U of Chicago P, 1944.

11 KLEIN, David. *The Elizabethan Dramatists as Critics.* New York: Philosophical Library, 1963.

12 KLEIN, Karl L. "Rhetorik und Dichtungslehre in der elisabethanischen Zeit." In *Festschrift zum 75. Geburtstage von Theodor Spira*, ed. Helmut Viebrock and Willi Erzgräber. Heidelberg: Winter, 1961, pp. 164–83.

13 MACCHIONI JODI, Rodolfo. "L'Imitazione nella poetica del Rinascimento." *Palatina*, 4(1960):106–9.

14 MARZOT, Giulio. *L'Ingengo e il genio de Seicento.* Florence, n.p., 1944.

15 MONTANO, Rocco. *L'Estetica del Renascimento e del Barocco.* Naples: Quaderni, 1962.

16 PARTREE, Morris Henry. "Plato and the Elizabethan Defense of Poetry." *DA*, 27(1966):459A–560A (Tex).

17 RAYMOND, Marcel. *Baroque et Renaissance poétique.* Paris: Corti, 1955.*

18 ROMUALDEZ, Antonio V. "Towards a History of the Renaissance Idea of Wisdom." *SRen*, 11(1964):133–50.

19 ROSSKY, William. "Imagination in the English Renaissance: Psychology and Poetic." *SRen*, 5(1958):49–73.

20 RUBEL, Veré Laura. *Poetic Diction in the English Renaissance from Skelton through Spenser.* New York: MLA, 1941.

21 RUSSO, Luigi. "La Poetica di Platone e il Rinascimento." *Belfagor*, 16(1961):401–15.

22 SAULNIER, Verdun L. *La Littérature française de la Renaissance.* 6th ed. rev. Paris: P U de France, 1962.

1   SCOTT, Izora. *Controversies over Imitation of Cicero as a Model for Style and Some Phases of Their Influence on the Schools of the Renaissance.* New York: Teachers College, 1910. [Includes translation of Erasmus' *Ciceronius.*]

2   SHEPARD, Sanford. *El Pinciano y las teorías literarias del Siglo de Oro.* Madrid: Gredos, 1962.

3   SIMON, Irène. "Critical Terms in Restoration Translations from the French." *RBPH*, 42(1965):902–26.

4   SMITH, A. J. "Theory and Practice in Renaissance Poetry: Two Kinds of Imitation." *BJRL*, 47(1964):212–43.

5   SMITH, George Gregory. See 2.13.

6   SOWTON, Ian. "Hidden Persuaders as a Means of Literary Grace: Sixteenth-Century Poetics and Rhetoric in England." *UTQ*, 32(1962):55–69.

7   SPINGARN, Joel Elias. *La Critica letteraria nel Rinascimento, saggio sulle origini dello spirito classico nella letteratura moderna,* trans. Antonio Fusco, with corrections and additions by the author and preface by B. Croce. Bari: Laterza, 1950. [Italian edition of 2.15, revised by the author, and including a preface by Benedetto Croce.]*

8   ———. *A History of Literary Criticism in the Renaissance.* 2nd ed. New York: Columbia U P, 1963. [Columbia University Studies in Comparative Literature.] [Harbinger-H025]†

9   STEADMAN, John M. "Verse Without Rime: Sixteenth-Century Italian Defenses of *Versi Sciolti.*" *Italica*, 41(1964):384–402.

10   SWEETING, Elizabeth Jane. *Earl Tudor Criticism, Linguistic and Literary.* New York: Russell and Russell, 1964.

11   TALBERT, Ernest William. *Elizabethan Drama and Shakespeare's Early Plays: An Essay in Historical Criticism.* Chapel Hill: U of North Carolina P, 1963.

12   TAYLER, Edward William. See 2.16.

13   ———. *Nature and Art in Renaissance Literature.* New York: Columbia U P, 1964.

14   ———. "Nature and Art in the English Renaissance: Some Literary Consequences of a Philosophic Idea." *DA*, 21(1961):2279–80 (Stan).

15   THALER, Alwin. "Literary Criticism in *A Mirror for Magistrates.*" *JEGP*, 49:1–13.

16   THOMPSON, Guy Andrew. *Elizabethan Criticism of Poetry.* Menasha, Wis.: Banta, 1914.

17   TIGERSTEDT, E. N. "Observations on the Reception of the Aristotelian *Poetics* in the Latin West." *SRen*, 15(1968):7–24.

18   TRABALZA, Ciro. *La Critica letteraria nel Rinascimento.* Milan: Vallardi, 1915.

19   TUVE, Rosamond. *Elizabethan and Metaphysical Imagery: Renaissance Poetic and Twentieth-Century Critics.* Chicago: U of Chicago P, 1957. [Phoenix-P68].†

1   VILANOVA, Antonio. "Preceptistas españoles de los siglos XVI y XVIII." In *Historia general de las literaturas hispánicas*, ed. Barna. Barcelona, 1953. Vol. 3, pp. 567–691.

2   VOSSLER, Karl. *Poetische Theorien in der italienischen Frührenaissance.* Berlin: Felber, 1900.*

3   WEINBERG, Bernard. See 2.17.

4   ———. *A History of Literary Criticism in the Italian Renaissance.* 2 vols. Chicago: U of Chicago P, 1963.*

5   ———. "Poetry and Poetic Theory in the Italian Renaissance." *UTQ*, 31(1962):283–98.

6   ———. "The Problem of Literary Aesthetics in Italy and France in the Renaissance." *MLQ*, 14:448–56.

7   WELLEK, René. "Concept of Baroque in Literary Scholarship." *JAAC*, 5:77–109. [Reprinted in his *Concepts of Criticism.* See 7.4.*]

8   WHITE, Harold Ogden. *Plagiarism and Imitation During the English Renaissance: A Study in Critical Distinctions.* New York: Octagon, 1965. [Harvard Studies in English, 12.]

9   WILLIAMS, Ralph C. "Italian Critical Treatises of the Sixteenth Century." *MLN*, 35(1920):506–7.

10   WILSON, Harold S. "Some Meanings of 'Nature' in Renaissance Literary Theory." *JHI*, 2(1941):430–48.

11   WITTKOWER, Rudolf. "Individualism in Art and Artists: A Renaissance Problem." *JHI*, 22:291–302.

12   WOOD, Glena Decker. "Retributive Justice: A Study of the Theme of Elizabethan Revenge Tragedy." *DA*, 24(1963):2466–67 (Ky).

Individual Authors

Barthélemy Aneau

13   *Le Quintil Horatian sur la deffence et illustration de la langue françoise.* N.p. 1550.

Roger Ascham

14   *English Works: Toxophilus; Report of the Affaires and State of Germany; The Scholemaster*, ed. W. A. Wright. Cambridge: U P, 1904.

15   " 'Of Imitation': *The Scholemaster* (Book II)." *ECE*, 1:1–47. [1570.]

16   *The Scholemaster.* London: John Daye, 1570.

*   *   *

17   RYAN, Lawrence V. *Roger Ascham.* Stanford: Stanford U P, 1963.

Francis Bacon

1 *The Advancement of Learning*, ed. G. W. Kitchin. New York: Dutton, 1954. [Everyman's Library.]

2 "From The Advancement of Learning." *CESC*, 1:1–9. [1605.]

3 *The Two Bookes of Francis Bacon: Of the Proficience and Aduancement of Learning, Diuine and Humane.* 2 parts. London: For Henrie Tomes, 1605.

* * *

4 KOCHER, Paul H. "Francis Bacon on the Drama." In *Essays on Shakespeare and Elizabethan Drama in Honor of Hardin Craig.* Columbia: U of Missouri P, 1962, pp. 297–307.

5 WALLACE, Karl R. *Francis Bacon on Communication and Rhetoric.* Chapel Hill: U of North Carolina P, 1943.

Jean-Antoine de Baïf

6 *Etrénes de poézie fransoeze an vers mesurés.* Paris, 1574.

7 *Oeuvres en rime*, ed. Ch. Marty-Laveaux. 5 vols. Paris, 1881–90.

Lazare de Baïf

8 *Dédicace au Roy* to *Hécube*, tragedy translated from Euripedes. Paris, 1544.

9 *Diffinition de la tragédie, Préface* to *Électre*, translated from Sophocles. Paris, 1537.

Pietro Bembo

10 *Le Prose della volgar lingua.* Venice, 1525.

11 *Prose della volgar lingua.* Torino: UTET, 1931.

12 *Prose e rime*, ed. Carlo Dionisotti. Turin: UTET, 961.

* * *

13 PETTENATI, Gastone. "Il Bembo sul valore delle 'Lettere' e Dionisio d'Alicarnasso." *SFI*, 18(1960):69–77.

Paolo Beni

14 *Comparationi di Homero, Virgilio e Torquato, e chi di loro si debba la palma nell'heroico poema.* Padua, 1607.

15 *In Aristotelis poeticam commentarii.* Padua, 1613.

Giovanni Boccaccio

16 *Boccaccio on Poetry*, trans. Charles G. Osgood. Princeton: Princeton U P, 1930. [LLA 82]†

1 "The Life of Dante." *LC*, pp. 208–11. [Selections.]
   Vita di Dante. Bari, 1918.

2 ˙ *Vita di Dante e Difesa della poesia*, ed. Carlo Muscetta. Rome: Ateneo, 1962.

Giordano Bruno

3 *Degli eroici furiori*, al molto illustre ed excellente cavaliere Signor Filippo Sidneo. London, 1585.

4 "De gl'heroici furiori." In *Dialoghi italiani*, ed. Giovanni Aquilecchia. Florence: Sansoni, 1958.

*   *   *

5 BÀRBERI Squarotti, Giorgio. "Per una descrizione e interpretazione della poetica di Giordano Bruno." *SSe*, 1(1960):39–60.

6 YATES, Frances Amelia. *Giordano Bruno and the Hermetic Tradition*. London: Routledge and Kegan Paul, 1964.

Francesco Buonamici

7 *Discorsi poetici in difesa d'Aristotile*. Florence, 1597.

Thomas Campion

8 *Observations in the Art of English Poesie*. London: Andrew Wise, 1602.

9 "Observations in the Art of English Poesie." *ECE*, 2:327–55.

Nausea Blancacampiano Campiano

10 *In artem poeticam primordia*. Venice, 1522.

Giovanni Pietro Capriano

11 *Della vera poetica, libro uno*. Venice, 1555.

Richard Carew

12 "The Excellency of the English Tongue." *ECE*, 2:285–94. [1595–96?]

Luis Carrillo y Sotomayor

1 *Libro de la erudición poética*. Madrid: Juan de la Cuesta, 1611.

2 *Libro de la erudición poética*, ed. Manuel Cardenal Iracheta. Madrid: Aguirre, 1946.

3 *El Pasajero*, ed. Francisco Rodriguez Marin. Madrid, 1913. [1611.]

Annibale Caro

4 *Apologia degli Academici di Banchi di Roma contra messer Lodovico Castelvetro*. Parma, 1558.

Giambattista Casalio

5 *De tragoedia et comoedia lucubratio*. In Vol. 8 of Jacobus Gronovius, *Thesaurus graecarum antiquitatum*. 13 vols. Leyden, 1697–1702.

Ludovico Castelvetro

6 "A Commentary on the *Poetics* of Aristotle." *LC*, pp. 305–57. [Selections trans. by A. H. Gilbert.]

7 *Opere varie critiche: Colla vita dell' autore*, ed. L. A. Muratori. Lyons, 1727.

8 *Poetica d'Aristotele vulgarizzata et sposta*. 2d ed. Basel, 1576.

9 *Ragione d'alcune cose segnate nella canzone d'Annibal Caro*. Modena, 1559–60.

*   *   *

10 BREITINGER, H. "Un Passage de Castelvetro sur l'unité de lieu." *Revue critique d'histoire et de littérature*, n.s. 7(1879):478–80.

11 CHARLETON, Henry Buckley. *Castelvetro's Theory of Poetry*. Manchester: U P, 1913.

12 FUSCO, Antonio. *La Poetica di Lodovico Castelvetro*. Naples, 1904.

13 MELZI, Robert C. *Castelvetro's Annotations to the "Inferno": A New Perspective in Sixteenth Century Criticism*. The Hague: Mouton, 1966. [Studies in Italian Literature, 1.] [Humanities]

14 WEINBERG, Bernard. "Castelvetro's Theory of Poetics." *C&C*, pp. 349–71.

Ridolfo Castravilla

15 *I Discorsi di Ridolfo Castravilla contro Dante e di Filippo Sassetti in difesa di Dante, annotazioni di Bellisario Bulgarini*. Siena, 1608. [1570?]

16 *I Discorsi di Ridolfo Castravilla contro Dante*, ed. Mario Rossi. Castello: Lapi, 1897.

Bartolomeo Cavalcanti

1 *Giudicio sopra la tragedia di Canace e Macareo (di Sperone Speroni degli Alvarotti) con molte utili considerazioni circa l'arte tragica et di altri poemi con la tragedia appresa.* Venice, 1566.

2 *La Retorica di M. Bartolomeo Cavalcanti.* Venice: Appresso G. Gidito de'Ferrari, 1559.

Miguel de Cervantes

3 [Miguel de Cervantes Saavedra.] *Viaje del Parnaso.* Madrid, 1614.

* * *

4 GARCÍA, F. Olmos. "Ideas de Cervantes sobre la función de la literatura y la misión del autor." *LT*, 228(1965):92–105.

5 RILEY, E. C. *Cervantes's Theory of the Novel.* Oxford: Clarendon P, 1962.

George Chapman

6 "The Dedication of *The Revenge of Bussy D'Ambois.*" *LC*, pp. 549–50. [c. 1611.] [In part.]

7 "Preface to *Seaven Bookes of the Iliades of Homere.*" *ECE*, 2:295–97. [1598.]

8 "Prefaces to the Translation of Homer." *CESC*, 1:67–81. [1610–16?]

* * *

9 HERRING, Thelma. "Chapman and an Aspect of Modern Criticism." *RenD*, 8(1965):153–79.

Mathieu Coignet

10 "From *Politique Discourses*," trans. Sir E. Hoby. *ECE*, 1:339–44. [1586.]

Samuel Daniel

11 "A Defence of Rhyme." *ECE*, 2:356–84. [1603?]

12 *Poems and A Defense of Ryme*, ed. A. C. Sprague. Chicago: U of Chicago P, 1965. [Phoenix-P200]†

* * *

13 JOHNSON, Marsue McFaddin. "The Well-Rimed Daniel: An Examination of *Delia* and *A Defence of Ryme.*" *DA*, 26(1966):4661 (Ark).

Bernardino Daniello

1   *La Poetica.* Venice, 1536.

Bernardo Davanzati

2   *Le Opere*, ed. E. Bindi. Florence: Le Monier, 1888.

3   *Scisma d'Inghilterra, con altre operette.* 1st Florentine ed. 1638. 2d ed. entirely like 1st. Padua: Comino, 1754.

4   *Lo Scisma d'Inghilterra, con un discorso di Enrico Bindi intorno la vita e le opere dell' autore.* Milan: Instituto Editoriale Italiano, 19– . [New Library of Italian Classics. Ser. 2, vol. 34.]

Pierre de Deimier

5   *L'Académie de l'art poétique . . . oeuvre non moins exacte et requise pour les reigles et observations du bien dire, comme pour l'intelligence de l'art poétique françois.* Paris, 1610.

Jason de Nores

6   *Apologia, contra l'autore del Verato di Giason de Nores di quanto ha egli detto in suo discorso delle tragicomedie, & delle pastorale.* Padua, 1590.

7   *Discorso intorno a que' principii che la comedia, la tragedia, e il poema heroica ricevano dalla philosophia morale e civile e da governatori delle repubbliche.* Padua, 1587.

8   *In epistolam Q. Horatii Flacci de Arte Poetica . . . interpretatio. Eiusdem brevis, ex distincta summa praeceptorum de arte dicendi ex tribus Ciceronis libris de Oratore Collecta.* Venice, 1553.

9   *Poetica nella qual si tratta secondo l'opinione d'Aristotle della tragedia, del poema heroica, e della comedia.* Padua, 1588.

Lodovico Dolce

10   *Horace's Ars Poetica*, translated with commentary. Venice, 1535.

Estienne Dolet

11   *La Manière de bien traduire d'une langue en aultre.* Lyon: Dolet, 1540

12   "La Manière de bien traduire d'une langue en aultre." *CP*, pp. 77–83.

Michael Drayton

1   "Epistle to Henry Reynolds, of Poets and Poesy." *CESC*, 1:134–40. [1627.]

Joachim du Bellay

2   *La Deffence et illustration de la langue françoise.* Paris, 1549.

3   *La Defense et illustration de la langue française*, ed. Henri Chamard. Paris: Didier, 1948. [Sociéte des Textes Français Modernes.]

4   *The Defence and Illustration of the French Language*, trans. Gladys M. Turquet. London: Dent, 1939.

5   "Preface to *L'Olive.*" *CP*, pp. 139–40. [1549.]

6   "Second Preface to *L'Olive.*" *CP*, pp. 153–60. [1550.]

*   *   *

7   DASSONVILLE, Michel. "De l'unité de la *Deffence et illustration de la langue françoyse*." *BHR*, 27(1965):96–107.

Richard Edwards

8   "Prologue to Damon and Pythias." In *The Dramatic Writings of Richard Edwards, Thomas Norton, and Thomas Sackville*, ed. John S. Farmer. New York: Barnes and Noble, 1966.

Sir Thomas Elyot

9   *The Book Named the Governor*, ed. S. E. Lehmberg. New ed. New York: Dutton, 1962. [Everyman's Library.]

10   *The Boke Named the Gouernour*, ed. from the 1st ed. [1531] by H. H. S. Croft. 2 vols. New York: Franklin, 1967.

11   *Of that Knowlage which Maketh a Wise Man.* London: Berthelet, 1534. [1533.]

12   *Of that Knowledge which Maketh a Wise Man*, ed. Edwin Johnston Howard. Oxford, Ohio: Anchor P, 1946.

*   *   *

13   HOGREFE, Pearl. "Sir Thomas Elyot's Intention in the Opening Chapters of the *Governour*." *SP*, 60(1963):133–40.

1 MAJOR, John M. *Sir Thomas Elyot and Renaissance Humanism.* Lincoln: U of Nebraska P, 1964.

Juan del Encina

2 *Arte de la poesía castellano.* Madrid, 1496.

Charles Estienne

3 *Épistre au Dauphin, Préface* to *Les Abusez,* translation of the Italian comedy *Gl'ingannati,* a collective work. Paris, 1543.

Henri Estienne

4 *Conformité du langage françois avec le grec.* Geneva, 1565.

5 *Deux dialogues du nouveau langage françois italianizé et autrement desguizé.* Geneva, 1578.

6 *La Précellence du langage françois,* ed. Edmond Huguet. Paris, 1896.

7 *Project du livre intitulé la Précellence du langage françois.* Paris, 1579.

Pierre Fabri

8 *Le Grand et vray art de pleine rhétorique.* Rouen, 1521.

9 *Le Grand et vrai art de pleine rhétorique,* ed. A. Heron. 3 vols. Rouen: Cagniard, 1889–90.

Marsilio Ficino

10 KRISTELLER, Paul Oskar. *The Philosophy of Marsilio Ficino,* trans. Virginia Conont. New York: Columbia U P, 1943. [Repr. Gloucester, Mass.: Smith, 1964.]

Publio Fontana

11 *Del proprio ed ultimo fine del poeta.* Bergamo, 1615.

Girolamo Fracastoro

12 *Naugerius, sive de poetica dialogus.* Venice, 1584. [1555.]

13 *Naugerius: sive, De poetica dialogus,* trans. Ruth Kelso. Urbana: U of Illinois P, 1924. [Latin and English.] [ISLL, 9.]

Abraham Fraunce

1 *The Arcadian Rhetorike*, edited from the original ed. of 1588 by Ethel Seaton. Oxford: For the Luttrell Society by Blackwell, 1950.

2 "From *The Arcadian Rhetorike*." *ECE*, 1:303–6. [1588.]

Galileo Galilei

3 *Considerazioni al Tasso*. Rome and Venice, 1793. [ca. 1600.]

4 *Postille all'Ariosto*. Vol. 9 of *Le Opere di Galileo Galilei*. National Edition under the auspices of His Majesty, the King of Italy. 20 vols. Florence: Tip. di G. Barbèra, 1890–1909. ica. 1600.]

* * *

5 DELLA TERZA Dante. "Galileo letterato: *Considerazioni al Tasso*." *RLI*, 49(1965):77–91.

Diego García Rengifo

6 [Juan Dias Rengifo.] *Arte poética española*. Barcelona: Martí, 1759. [1592.]

Robert Garnier

7 *Oeuvres complètes, théâtre et poésies*, ed. L. Pinvert. Paris: Garnier, 1923.

George Gascoigne

8 "Certayne Notes of Instruction." *ECE*, 1:46–57. [1575.]

* * *

9 MODIC, John L. "Gascoigne and Ariosto Again." *CL*, 14(1962):317–19.

Lorenzo Giacomini

10 [Lorenzo Giacomini Tebalducci Malespini.] *Orazioni e discorsi de Lorenzo Giacomini Tebalducci Malespini*. Florence: Sermartelli, 1597. [For literary criticism see especially "De la purgatione de la tragedia," "Del furor poetico."]

Andrea Gilio da Fabriano

1   *La Topica poetica.* Venice, 1580.

Lilio Gregorio Giraldi

2   *Dialogi duo de poetis nostrorum temporum.* Florence, 1551.

Giambattista Giraldi Cinthio

3   "An Address to the Reader by the Tragedy of *Orbecche.*" *LC*, pp. 243–46. [1541.] [In English.]

4   "The Apology for *Dido.*" *LC*, pp. 246–52. [1543.] [In part.]

5   Dedication of *Orbecca, tragedia.* Venice?, 1541.

6   *Discorsi intorno al comporre dei romanzi delle commedie, e delle tragedie.* Venice, 1554.

7   *Discorso sulle comedie e sulle tragedie.* Venice?, 1543.

8   "On the Composition of Comedies and Tragedies." *LC*, pp. 252–62. [1543.] [Selections.]

9   "On the Composition of Romances:" *LC*, pp. 262–73. [1549.] [Selections.]

10 *Scritti estetici: De'romanzi, delle comedie e della tragedie.* 2 vols. Milan, 1864. [Biblioteca Rara de Daelli, Nos. 51–52.]

11 *Le Tragedie.* Venice, 1583.

*   *   *

12 CROCETTI, Camillo Guerrieri. *G. B. Giraldi ed il pensiero critico del secolo XVI.* Milan: Albright, Segati, 1932.

Baltasar Gracián

13 *Agudeza y arte de ingenio.* Madrid: Juan Sánchez, 1648. [1642.]

14 *Agudeza y arte de ingenio.* Madrid: Rafa, 1929.

*   *   *

15 BETHELL, S. L. "The Nature of Metaphysical Wit." In *Discussions of John Donne*, ed. Frank Kermode. Boston: Heath, 1962.

16 CROCE, Benedetto. "I Trattatisi italiani del concettismo e Baltasar Gracián." In his *Problemi di estetica.* 4th ed. Bari: Laterza, 1949.

17 HEGER, Klaus. *Baltasar Gracián: Estilo y doctrina.* Saragossa: Inst. Fernando el Católico, 1960.

18 LACOSTA, Francisco C. "El Conceptismo barroco de Baltasar Gracián en *Arte y agudeza de ingenio.*" *RR*, 55(1964):85–90.

Jacques Grévin

1 *Brief discours pour l'intelligence de ce théâtre.* Paris, 1562. [Preface to the tragedy *La Mort de César.*]

2 *Théâtre complet et poésies choisies,* ed. L. Pinvert. Paris: Garnier, 1922. [For literary criticism see especially his prefaces.]

Giacopo Grifoli

3 *Q. Horatii Flacci de Arte poetica . . . explicatio.* Florence, 1550.

Giambattista Guarini

4 *Compendio della poesia tragicomica, tratto dai due Verati.* Venice, 1603.

5 "The Compendium of Tragicomic Poetry." *LC*, pp. 505–33. [1601.] [In part.]

6 *Difesa di quanto ha scritto Giasone Denores contra le tragicommedie e le pastorali in su discorso di poesie.* Ferrara, 1588.

7 *Il Pastor Fido e il compendio della poesia tragicomica.* Bari, 1914.

8 *Il Pastor Fido: A Critical Edition of Sir Richard Fanshawe's 1647 Translation,* ed. Walter F. Staton, Jr., and William E. Simeone. Oxford: Clarendon P, 1964.

9 *Replica dell'Altizzato Academico Ferrarese in difesa del Pastor Fido.* Florence, 1593.

Sir John Harington

10 "Preface to Orlando Furioso." *ECE*, 2:194–222. [1591.]

*   *   *

11 ELLRODT, R. "Sir John Harington and Leone Ebreo." *MLN*, 65(1950): 109–10.

Gabriel Harvey

12 "From *A New Letter of Notable Contents.*" *ECE*, 2:282–84. [1593.]

13 "From *Pierce's Supererogation.*" *ECE*, 2:245–82. [1593.]

14 *Marginalia,* ed. G. C. Moore Smith. Stratford: Shakespeare Head, 1913.

Daniel Heinsius

1   *De tragoediae constitutione liber, in quo, inter caetera, tota de hac Aristotelis sententia dilucide explicatur.* Leyden, 1611.

* * *

2   SELLIN, Paul R. *Daniel Heinsius and Stuart England.* London: Oxford U P, 1968.

Fernando de Herrera

3   "Anotaciones." In Garcilaso de la Vega, *Obras.* Seville: Alonso de la Barrera, 1580.

Thomas Heywood

4   *An Apology for Actors.* London, 1814. [1612.] [Reprinted for the Shakespeare Society.]

5   "An Apology for Actors." *LC*, pp. 553–64. [1612.] [Selections.]

James I

6   [James VI of Scotland. James I of Great Britain.] "Ane Schort Treatise Conteining Some Reulis and Cautelis to be Observit and Eschewit in Scottis Poesie." *ECE*, 1:208–25. [1584.]

7   *Essayes of a Prentise in the Divine Art of Poesie.* Edinburgh, 1585. [English Reprints, ed. Edward Arber, 19.]

Juan de Juaregui

8   *Discurso poético.* Madrid: Juan González, 1624. [1623.] [Also in J. J. de Urriés, *Biografía y estudio crítico de Jauregui*, pp. 220–60. See 39.9.]

* * *

9   URRIÉS, José Jordán de. *Biografía y estudio crítico de Jauregui.* Madrid: Rivadeneyra, 1899.

Ben Jonson

10   *Conversations with Drummond of Hawthornden*, ed. R. F. Patterson. London: Blackie, 1923. [1619.]

11   "From *Every Man In His Humour*." *ECE*, 2:387–90.

12   "From *Every Man Out of His Humour*." *ECE*, 2:390–93.

1 "From *The Poetaster*." *ECE*, 2:393–97.

2 "From *The Returne from Parnassus*." *ECE*, 2:398–403.

3 *Timber; or, Discoveries*, ed. Ralph Walker. Syracuse: Syracuse U P, 1953

4 *The Workes of Benjamin Jonson*. London: Will Stansby, 1616.

5 *Works*, ed. C. H. Herford and Percy Simpson. 11 vols. Oxford: Clarendon P, 1925–52. [For literary criticism see especially "To the Readers of *Sejanus*" and works cited separately above.]

*   *   *

6 BALDWIN, E. C. "Ben Jonson's Indebtedness to the Greek Character-Sketch." *MLN*, 16(1901):385–96.

7 FIELER, Frank B. "The Impact of Bacon and the New Science upon Jonson's Critical Thought in *Timber*." *RenP* (1958–60):84–92.

8 OVERALL, Frances Morgan Bernard. "Ben Jonson: A Study of His Comic Theory." *DA*, 23(1962):1352–53 (Vanderbilt).

9 PALMER, John. *Ben Jonson*. Port Washington, N.Y.: Kennikat P, 1967.

10 REDWINE, James Daniel. "Ben Jonson's Criticism of the Drama." *DA*, 24:4683–84 (Princeton).

11 ———. "Beyond Psychology: The Moral Basis of Jonson's Theory of Humor Characterization." *ELH*, 28(1961):316–34.

12 REINSCH, Hugo. *Ben Jonsons Poetik und seine Beziehungen zu Horaz·* Erlangen, 1899. [Münchener Beiträge zur romanischen und englischen Philologie, 16.]

13 SCHELLING, Felix Emmanuel. *Ben Jonson and the Classical School*. Baltimore: U of Pennsylvania 1898. [Also in *Shakespeare and "Demi-Science"*: *Papers on Elizabethan Topics*. Philadelphia: U of Pennsylvania P, 1927.]

14 SNUGGS, Henry L. "The Comic Humours: A New Interpretation." *PMLA*, 43:114–122.

15 ———. "The Source of Jonson's Definition of Comedy." *MLN*, 65(1950): 543–44.

16 SPINGARN, Joel E. "The Source of Jonson's *Discoveries*." *MP*, 2(1903): 1–10.

17 STEIN, Arnold. "Plain Style, Plain Criticism, Plain Dealing, and Ben Jonson." *ELH*, 30:306–16.

18 TRIMPI, Wesley. "Jonson and the Neo-Latin Authorities for the Plain Style." *PMLA*, 77(1962):21–26.

E. K.

19 [Edward Kirke.] "Epistle Dedicatory to *The Shepheardes Calender*." *ECE*, 1:127–34. [1579.]

Jean Vauquelin de La Fresnaye

20 *Art poétique*. Caen, 1605.

21 *Art poëtique françois*, ed. George Pellisier. Paris: Garnier, 1885.

22 "Preface to His *Satyres Françoises*." *CP*, pp. 271–76. [1605.]

Jean de La Taille

1 *De l'art de la tragédie*, ed. Fred West. Manchester: U of Manchester, 1939. [1572.]

2 "De l'art de la tragédie." *CP*, pp. 225–31.

3 "Dedication to Jacques de la Taille's *Daire*." *CP*, pp. 233–34. [1573.]

4 *La Manière de faire des vers en françois, comme en grec et en latin.* Paris, 1573.

5 "Prologue to *Les Corrivaux*." *CP*, pp. 235–36. [1573.]

*   *   *

6 HAN, Pierre. "Jacques de La Taille's *La Manière:* A Critical Edition." *DA*, 21 (1961):3450–51 (Colum).

Pierre de Laudun

7 *Art poétique françois.* Paris, 1598.

8 *L'Art poétique françois*, ed. J. Dedieu. Toulouse: Facultés Libres, 1909. [1597.]

Alessandro Lionardi

9 *Dialogi della inventione poetica.* Venice, 1554.

Thomas Lodge

10 "A Defence of Poetry." *ECE*, 1:61–86. [1579.]

Francesco Luisino

11 *In librum Q. Horatii Flacci de Arte Poetica commentarius.* Venice, 1544.

Vicenzo Maggi and Bartolomeo Lombardi

12 *In Q. Horatti Flacci de Arte Poetica interpretatio.* Venice, 1550.

13 *Objectiones adversus Robortelli explicationes in primum Aristotelis contextum.* Venice, 1550.

Paolo Aldo Manuzio

14 *Dionysii Longini de Sublime Genere Dicendi.* Venice, 1555.

15 *In Q. Horatii Flacci . . . librum de Arte Poetica . . . commentarius.* Venice, 1576.

Orazio Marta

1 *Spozitione della Poetica d'Aristotile.* Naples, 1616.

Philip Massinger

2 *The Roman Actor,* ed. William L. Sandidge. Princeton: Princeton U P, 1929. [1626.]

3 "The Roman Actor." *LC,* pp. 569–73. [Selections.]

Jacopo Mazzoni

4 *Della difesa della Commedia di Dante.* Cesena, 1587–88.

5 *Discorso in difesa della Commedia del divino poeta Dante,* ed. Mario Rossi. Citta di Castello, 1898. [1572.]

6 "A Discourse in Defense of the *Comedy* of Dante." *LC,* p. 359. [Selection.]

7 "On the Defense of the *Comedy.*" *LC,* pp. 359–403. [Selections.]

* * *

8 BARBI, Michele. *La Fortuna di Dante nel secolo XVI.* Florence, 1890.*

Lorenzo dè Medici

9 *Commento di Lorenzo de' Medici sopra alcuni de suoi sonetti.* Venice, 1554.

Francis Meres

10 *Francis Meres' Treatise "Poetrie": A Critical Edition,* ed Don Cameron Allen. Urbana: U of Illinois P, 1933. [ISLL, 16, 3–4.]

11 "From *Palladis Tamia.*" *ECE,* 2:308–34. [1598.]

Michelangelo

12 [Michelangelo Buonarrati.] CLEMENTS, Robert John. *Michelangelo's Theory of Art.* New York: New York U P, 1961.

13 PANOFSKY, Erwin. "The Neoplatonic Movement and Michelangelo." In his *Studies in Iconology.* Oxford: Oxford U P, 1939, pp. 171–230.

Agostino Michele

14 *Discorso in cui contra l'opinione de tutti i più illustri scrittori del arte poetica chiaramente si dimostra come si possono scribere con molto lode le comedie e le tragedie in prosa.* Venice, 1592.

Antonio Sebastianio Minturno

15 *L'Arte poetica del Sig. A.M. nelle quale si contengono i precetti heroici, tragici, comici, satyrici e d'ogni altra poesia.* Venice, 1563.

1 "L'Arte poetica." *LC*, pp. 275–303. [1564.] [Selections.]

2 *De Poeta libri sex.* Venice, 1559.

*   *   *

3 WEINBERG, Bernard. "The Poetic Theories of Minturno." In *Studies in Honor of Frederick W. Shipley.* St. Louis, 1942, pp. 101–29. [Washington University Studies, n.s. Language and Literature, 3.]

Le Père Mourgues

4 *Traité de la poésie françoise.* 1684.

Girolamo Muzio

5 "Dell'arte poetica." In *Rime Diverse del Mvtio Ivstinopolitano.* Venice: Appresso Gabriel Giolito de Ferrari e Fratelle, 1551. Fols. 68–94v.

6 *Tre libri di arte poetica, Tre libri di lettere in rime sciolte.* Venice, 1551.

Thomas Nash

7 "From *Strange Newes, or Foure Letters Confuted.*" *ECE*, 2:239–44. [1592.]

8 "From *The Anatomie of Absurdities.*" *ECE*, 1:321–37. [1589.]

9 "Preface to Greene's *Menaphon.*" *ECE*, 1:307–20. [1589.]

10 "Preface to Sidney's *Astrophel and Stella.*" *ECE*, 2:223–28. [1591.]

*   *   *

11 HIBBARD, G. R. *Thomas Nashe: A Critical Introduction.* Cambridge, Mass.: Harvard U P, 1962.

Martin Opitz

12 "The Book Concerning German Poetry," trans. Olga Marz Perlzweig. *LC*, pp. 565–67. [1624.] [Selections.]

13 *Buch von der deutschen Poeterey, 1624,* ed. T. W. Braune. Tübingen: Niemeyer, 1963. [Facsim. of 1870 ed.]

*   *   *

14 BERGHOEFFER, W. *Martin Opitz, Buch von der deutschen Poeterei.* Frankfurt, 1886.

Bernardino Parthenio

15 *De poetica imitatione libri quinque.* Venice, 1565.

16 *Della imitatione poetica.* Venice, 1560.

Francesco Patrizi

1   *Della poetica.* Ferrara, 1586.

Jacques Peletier du Mans

2   *L'Art poétique de Jacques Peletier du Mans*, ed. A. Boulanger. Paris: Les Belles Lettres, 1930. [1555.]

3   *Préface á l'Art poétique d'Horace.* Paris, 1547.

4   "Prefaces to Horace's *Ars Poetica.*" *CP*, pp. 111–15. [1545.]

Matteo Pellegrini

5   *Delle acutezze.* Genoa: Ferroni, 1639.

Camillo Pellegrino

6   *Il Caraffa overo dell'epica poesia dialogo (Tasso vs. Ariosto).* Florence?, 1583.

7   *Discorso della poetica.* Venice, 1618.

8   *Replica alla riposta degli Academici della Crusca, fatta contra il Dialogo dell'Epica Poesia come e' dicono dell'Orlando Furioso.* Mantua, 1586.

Alessandro Piccolomini

9   *Annotationi . . . nell libro della Poetica d'Aristotele: Con la traduttione del medesimo libro, in lingua volgare.* Venice, 1575.

Giovanni Pigna

10   [Giovanni Battista Nicolucci Pigna.] *I Romanzi.* Venice, 1554.

George Puttenham

11   [Richard Puttenham?] "The Arte of English Poesie." *ECE*, 2:1–193. [1589.]

12   *George Puttenham, The Arte of English Poesie*, ed. Gladys D. Willcock and Alice Walker. Cambridge: U P, 1936.

Peter Ramus

13   DUHAMEL, P. A. "The Logic and Rhetoric of Peter Ramus." *MP*, 46(1949):163–71.

1   HOWELL, Wilbur Samuel. "Ramus and English Rhetoric, 1574–1681." *QJS*, 37(1951):299–310.

2   ONG, Walter J. "Ramus and the Transit to the Modern Mind." *The Modern Schoolman*, 32(1955):307–9.

3   ———. *Ramus, Method, and the Decay of Dialogue*. Cambridge, Mass.: Harvard U P, 1958.

Bartolomeo Ricci

4   *De imitatione libri tres*. Venice, 1541.

Antonio Riccoboni

5   *Praecepta Aristotelis cum praecepta Horatii collata*. Padua, 1592.

Francesco Robortelli

6   *In librum Aristotelis de Arte Poetica explicationes*. Florence: Laurentium Torrentium, 1548.

*   *   *

7   WEINBERG, Bernard. "Robortelli on the *Poetics*." *C&C*, pp. 319–48

Pierre de Ronsard

8   *L'Abrégé de l'art poétique*. Paris, 1565

9   *L'Abrégé de l'art poétique*. London: Hacon and Ricketts, 1930.

10 "Abbregé de l'art poëtique françois." *CP*, pp. 196–210.

11 "A Brief on the Art of French Poetry," trans. James Harry Smith.   *GC*, pp. 179–86.

12 "First Preface to *La Franciade*." *CP*, pp. 219–23. [1572.

13 "Preface to His *Odes*." *CP*, pp. 145–48. [1550.]

14 *Première préface à La Franciade*. Paris, 1572.

15 "Third Preface to *La Franciade*." *CP*, pp. 253–69. [1587.]

16 *Troisième préface à La Franciade*. Paris, 1587.

*   *   *

17 BLECHMANN, Wilhelm. "*Imitatio creatrix* bei Ronsard." *ZFSL*, 73(1963): 1–16.

18 RAYMOND, Marcel. *L'Influence de Ronsard sur la poésie française (1550–1585)*. New ed. Geneva: Droz, 1965.

19 STACKLEBERG, Jürgen von. "Ronsard und Aristoteles." *BHR*, 25(1963): 349–61.

Niccolò Rossi

1   *Discorsi intorno alla commedia.* Venice, 1589.

2   *Discorsi intorno alla tragedia.* Venice, 1590.

Lionardo Salviati

3   *Degli accademici della Crusca difesa dell'Orlando Furioso dell'Ariosto Contra'l Dialogo dell'Epica Poesia di Camillo Pellegrino.* Florence, 1584.

Cristóbal Saurez de Figueroa

4   *El Pasajero.* Madrid: Luis Sánchez, 1617.

5   *El Pasajero*, ed. Justo García Morales, with prologue and notes. Madrid: Aguilar, 1945.

Girolamo Savonarola

6   [Girolamo Maria Francesco Matteo Savonarola.] *In poeticen apologeticus*, or *Apologetica del poetare.* Florence, 1534.

Julius Caesar Scaliger

7   "Contra poetices calumniatores declamatis." In his *Epistolae et orationes.* Leyden, 1600.

8   *Poetices libri septem.* Lyons, 1561.

9   *Select Translations from Scaliger's Poetics*, ed. Frederick M. Padelford. New York: Holt, 1905. [YSE, 26.]

*　　*　　*

10   CONSTANZO, Mario. "Introduzione alla poetica di Giulio Cesare Scaligero." *GSLI*, 138(1961):1–38.

11   HALL, Vernon. *Life of Julius Caesar Scaliger, 1484–1558.* Transactions of the American Philosophical Society. Philadelphia, 1950.

12   ———. "Scaliger's Defense of Poetry." *PMLA*, 63(1948):1125–30.

13   WEINBERG, Bernard. "Scaliger versus Aristotle on Poetics." *MP*, 39(1941–42):337–60.

Thomas Sebillet

14   *Art poétique françois.* Paris, 1548.

15   *Art poétique françois*, ed. Félix Gaiffe. Paris: Droz, 1932. [Société des Textes Français Modernes.]

1 "Epistre aux lecteurs" to *L'Iphigénie d'Euripide poëte tragiq: Tourné de Grec en François par l'auteur de L'Art poëtique.* Paris, 1549.

2 "Preface to Euripides' *Iphigenia.*" *CP*, pp. 141–44.

Agnolo Segni

3 *Ragionamento di M. Agnolo Segni . . . sopra le cose pertinenti alla poetica.* Florence: Marescotti, 1581.

Sir Philip Sidney

4 *An Apologie for Poetrie.* London: For Henry Olney, 1595.

5 *An Apology for Poetry; or, The Defense of Poesy*, ed. Geoffrey Shepherd. New York: Barnes and Noble, 1965. [Nelson's Medieval and Renaissance Library.]

6 *Prose Works*, ed. Albert Feuillerat. 4 vols. Cambridge, U P, 1962.

* * *

7 BAROWAY, Israel. "Tremellius, Sidney and Biblical Verse." *MLN*, 49:145–49.

8 BRONOWSKI, Jacob. *The Poet's Defence.* Cleveland: World, 1966.

9 DOWLIN, Cornell M. "Sidney and Other Men's Thoughts." *RES*, 20(1944): 257–71.

10 ———. "Sidney's Two Definitions of Poetry." *MLQ*, 3(1942):573–81.

11 DUHAMEL, P. A. "Sidney's *Arcadia* and Elizabethan Rhetoric." *SP*, 45(1948):134–50.

12 GOLDMAN, Marcus Selden. *Sir Philip Sidney and the Arcadia.* Urbana: U of Illinois P, 1934. [ISLL, 17, 1–2.]

13 HALLAM, George W. "Sidney's Supposed Ramism." *RenP*, 1963, pp. 11–20.

14 HATHAWAY, Baxter. See 25.22.

15 ISLER, Alan D. "Heroic Poetry and Sidney's Two *Arcadias.*" *PMLA*, 83(1968):368–80.

16 KROUSE, F. Michael. "Plato and Sidney's *Defense of Poesie.*" *CL*, 6(1954): 138–47.

17 MYRICK, Kenneth Orne. *Sir Philip Sidney as a Literary Craftsman.* 2d ed. Lincoln: U of Nebraska P, 1965.*

Edmund Spenser

18 "Letter to Sir Walter Raleigh." *LC*, pp. 463–65. [1589.] [In part.]

* * *

19 JONES, Harrie Stuart V. *A Spenser Handbook.* New York: Crofts, 1930.

Sperone Speroni

20 *La Canace, tragedia . . . alla quale sono aggiunte . . . alcune lettioni in difesa della tragedia.* Venice, 1597.

21 *I Dialoghi di Messer Sperone Speroni.* Venice, 1542.

Richard Stanyhurst

1 "From the Dedication and Preface to the Translation of the *Aeneid*." *ECE*, ed. 1:135–47. [1582.]

Faustino Summo

2 *Discorsi poetici . . . ne' quali si discorrono le più principali questioni di poesia, e si dichiarano molti luoghi dubi e difficili intorno all'arte di poetare; secondo la mente di Aristotele, di Platone, e di altri buoni autori.* Padua, 1600.

3 *Due discorsi: L'uno contra le tragicomedie e moderni pastorali, l'altro particolarmente contra il Pastor Fido, et insieme una risposta in difesa del metro nelle poesie e nei poemi.* Venice, 1601.

Bernardo Tasso

4 *Ragionamento della poesia.* Venice, 1562.

Torquato Tasso

5 *Apologia in difesa della sua Gerusalemme Liberata.* Ferrara, 1586.

6 *Discorsi dell'arte poetica e del poema eroico*, ed. Luigi Poma. Bari: Laterza, 1964.

7 *Discorso del poema eroico.* Naples, 1594.

8 *Discorso dell'arte poetica, ed in particolare del poema eroico.* Venice, 1587.

9 "Discourses on the Heroic Poem." *LC*, pp. 467–503. [Selections.]

10 *Gerusalemme liberata*, ed. Bruno Maier. Milan: Rizzoli, 1963.

11 *Jerusalem Delivered*, trans. Edward Fairfax, ed. Roberto Weiss. Carbondale: Southern Illinois U P, 1962. [Capricorn-77.]†

12 *Opere*, ed. B. T. Sozzi. New ed. Torino: UTET, 1964.

* * *

13 BOULTING, William. *Tasso and His Times.* London, 1907.

14 DA POZZO, Giovanni. "A proposito dei *Discorsi* del Tasso." *GSLI*, 142(1965):34–51.

15 RAGONESE, Gaetano. "Sui *Discorsi* del Tasso." *AFMag*, 2(1960–61):207–18.

16 RODITI, Edouard. "Torquato Tasso: The Transition from Baroque to Neo-Classicism." *JAAC*, 6(1948):235–45.

17 SIMPSON, Joyce C. *Le Tasse et la littérature et l'art baroques en France.* Paris: Nizet, 1962.

18 SOZZI, Bortolo Tommaso. "La Poetica del Tasso." *ST*, 5(1955):3–58.

Alessandro Tassoni

1 *Considerazioni sopra le Rime del Petrarca.* Modena: Cassiani, 1609.
2 *Opere,* ed. Giorgio Rossi. 2 vols. Bari, n.p. 1930.
3 *Pensieri diversi.* Modena, 1612.

* * *

4 ARCUDI, Bruno A. "A Seicento View of the *Divine Comedy.*" *Italica,* 43(1966):333–44.

Conte Emanuele Tesauro

5 *Il Cannocchiale aristotelico.* Venice, 1688. [1654.]

* * *

6 BETHELL, S. L. See 37.15.
7 BIANCHI, Dante. "Intorno al *Cannocchiale aristotelico.*" *Atti dell'Accademia ligure di scienze e lettere,* 17(1961):325–41.
8 DONATO, Eugenio. "Tesauro's Poetics: Through the Looking Glass." *MLN,* 78(1963):15–30.

Bonnell Thornton

9 McKILLOP, A. D. "Bonnell Thornton's Burlesque Ode." *N&Q,* 194(1949): 321–24.

Claudio Tolomei

10 *Versi e regole nella nuova poesia toscana.* Rome, 1539.

Bernardino Tomitano

11 *Annotationi nel libro della Poetica d'Aristotele.* Siena, 1570.

Giangiorgio Trissino

12 "Poetica." *LC,* pp. 213–32. [1529.] [Selections.]
13 *La Quinta e la sesta divisione della poetica.* Venice, 1563.
14 "Le Sei divisioni della poetica." In his *Tutte le opere.* Verona: J. Vallarsi, 1729.

* * *

1 HERRICK, Marvin T. "Trissino's *Art of Poetry*." In *Essays on Shakespeare and the Elizabethan Drama in Honor of Hardin Craig*, ed. Richard Hosley. Columbia: U of Missouri P, 1962, pp. 15–22.

2 MORSOLIN, Bernardo. *Giangiorgio Trissino*. Florence, 1894.

Pontus de Tyard

3 *Discours philosophiques: Solitaire premier, ou discours des muses et de la fureur poétique; Solitaire second, ou discours de la musique.* Lyons, 1552.

Benedetto Varchi

4 *L'Hercolano dialogo . . . nel qual si ragiona generalmente delle lingue, e in particulare della toscana e della fiorentina.* Florence, 1570.

5 *L'Ercolano e lezioni quattro sopra alcune questioni d'amore.* Milan: Sonzogno, 1880.

6 *Lezione della poetica in generale.* Florence, 1554.

*   *   *

7 MICHEL, Paul-Henri. "Problems of Artistic Creation: The Lesson of the Renaissance." *Diogenes*, 46:25–43.

8 PIROTTI, Umberto. "Benedetto Varchi e la questione della lingua." *Convivium*, 28(1960):524–52.

9 ———. "Benedetto Varchi e l'aristotelismo del Rinascimento." *Convivium*, 31(1963):280–311.

William Vaughn

10 "From *The Golden Grove*." *ECE*, 2:325–26. [1600.]

Lope de Vega

11 [Lope Félix de Vega Carpio.] "Arte nuevo de hacer comedias en este tiempo." In his *Rimas*. Madrid: Alonso Martín, 1621. [1609.]

12 "Arte nuevo de hacer comedias en este tiempo," ed. A. Morel-Fatio. *Bulletin Hispanique*, 3(1901):365–405.

13 "The New Art of Making Comedies," trans. Olga Marx Perlzweig. *LC*, pp. 541–48.

*   *   *

14 CRINÓ, Anna María. "Lope de Vega's Exertions for the Abolition of the Unities in Dramatic Practice." *MLN*, 76(1961):259–61.

Richard Verstegan

1   *A Restitution of Decayed Intelligence in Antiquities.* London: John Bill, 1628.

Piero Vettori

2   *Commentarii in primum librum Aristotelis de Arte Poetarum.* Florence, 1560.

Marco Girolamo Vida

3   *De arte poetica.* Cremona, 1527.

*   *   *

4   COOK, Albert S., ed. *The Art of Poetry.* See 1.7.

Gianantonio Viperano

5   *De poetica libri tres.* Antwerp, 1558.

Gerardus Joannes Vossius

6   *De artis poeticae natura ac constitutione.* Amsterdam, 1647.

William Webbe

7   "A Discourse of English Poetry." *ECE*, 1:226–302. [1586.]

George Whetstone

8   "The Dedication to *Promos and Cassandra.*" *ECE*, 1:58–60. [1578.]

Richard Willes

9   "From *Poematum Liber.*" *ECE*, 1:46–7. [1573.]

Thomas Wilson

10   *The Art of Rhetorike*, ed. G. H. Mair. Oxford: Clarendon P, 1909. [1560.]

11   *The Arte of Rhetorique, 1553*, ed. Robert Hood Bowers. Gainesville, Fla.: SF&R, 1962. [A facsim. reprod.]

*   *   *

12   WAGNER, Russell H. "Thomas Wilson's *Arte of Rhetorique.*" *SM*, 28(1960):1–32.

52

Gabriele Zinano

1   *Discorso della tragedie.* Reggio, 1590.

Girolamo Zoppio

2   *Ragionamenti in difesa di Dante e del Petrarca.* Bologna, 1583.

Later Criticism Through Johnson

General

3   ABRAMS, Meyer Howard. See 3.1.*

4   ACCOLTI, Gil Vitale, Nicola. *Verso la critica letteraria (Gottsched, Bodmer e Breitinger, Lessing).* Varese: Magenta, 1952.

5   ADAMS, Henry Hitch, and Baxter HATHAWAY. See 1.1.

6   AGATE, James E. See 1.2.

7   ALDRIDGE, A. O. "The Pleasures of Pity." *ELH*, 16(1949):76–87.

8   ARNOLD, Hans Stephen. "The Reception of Ben Jonson, Beaumont and Fletcher, and Massinger in Eighteenth-Century Germany." *DA*, 26(1965): 3323–24 (Md).

9   ATKINS, John William Hey. See 3.4.

10 BABCOCK, R. W. "The Idea of Taste in the Eighteenth Century." *PMLA*, 50(1935):922–26.

11 BATE, Walter Jackson. *From Classic to Romantic: Premises of Taste in Eighteenth-Century England.* New York: Harper, 1961. [Torchbooks-TB1036]†

12 ———. "The Sympathetic Imagination in Eighteenth-Century English Criticism." *ELH*, 12(1945):144–64.

13 BENZIGER, James. "Organic Unity: Leibniz to Coleridge." *PMLA*, 66(1951):24–48.

14 BIGI, Emilio. See 1.5.

15 BIHLER, Heinrich. *Spanische Verdichtung des Mittelalters im Lichte der spanischen Kritik der Aufklärung und Vorromantik.* Münster: Aschendorff, 1957.

16 BINNI, Walter. *Classicismo e neoclassicismo nella letteratura del Settecento.* Florence: Nuova Italia, 1963.

17 ———. "Poetica e poesia nel Settecento italiano." *RLI*, 66(1962):203–23.

18 BLOCK, Haskell M. "The Concepts of Imitation in Modern Criticism." *Proceedings of the IVth Congress of the International Comparative Literature Association.* The Hague: Mouton, 1966.*

1   BOERSCH, Alfred H. *"The Sense of Beauty, The Idea of Beauty,* and *The Beauty of Nature:* Theories of Beauty in England: 1700–1760." *DA,* 24(1963):1158–59 (Minn).

2   BOLDINI, Rinaldo. *Giacomo Bodmer e Pietro di Calepio incontro della "Scuola Svizzera" con il pensiero estetico italiano.* Milan: Società Editrice "Vita e Pensiero," 1953.

3   BOLGAR, R. R. *The Classical Heritage and Its Beneficiaries.* Cambridge: U P, 1954.

4   BOND, Donald F. "Distrust of Imagination in English Neo-Classicism." *PQ,* 14(1935):54–69.

5   BOND, Richmond P. *English Burlesque Poetry, 1700–1750.* Cambridge, Mass.: Harvard U P, 1932.

6   BORGERHOFF, E. O. *The Freedom of French Classicism.* Princeton: Princeton U P, 1950.

7   BORGLENGHI, Aldo. *La Critica letteraria nella prima metà dell'Ottocento.* Milan: Goliardica, 1960.

8   BOSKER, Aisso. *Literary Criticism in the Age of Johnson.* 2d ed. rev. Groningen: Wolters, 1954.

9   BOYD, J. D. See 3.15.

10 BRADY, Patrick. "Rococo and Impressionism: The Arts in France Before and After Romanticism, with Some Remarks as to the Importance of Non-Classical Values in French Culture." In *Proceedings of the Ninth Congress of the Australasian Universities' Languages and Literature Association, 19–26 August 1964,* ed. Marion Adams. Melbourne: U of Melbourne, 1964, pp. 76–78.

11 ———. "Rococo and Neo-Classicism." *SFr,* 8(1964), 34–49.

12 BRAY, René. *La Formation de la doctrine classique en France.* Dijon: Darantière, 1927. [Repr. 1951.]*

13 BREDVOLD, Louis I. *The Natural History of Sensibility.* Detroit: Wayne State U P, 1962. [WB9.]†

14 ———. "The Tendency Toward Platonism in Neo-Classical Esthetics." *ELH,* 1(1934):91–119.

15 BRETT, R. L. "The Aesthetic Sense and Taste in Literary Criticism of the Early Eighteenth Century." *RES,* 20(1944):199–213.

16 BRYSON, Gladys. *Man and Society: The Scottish Inquiry of the Eighteenth Century.* Princeton: Princeton U P, 1945.

17 BULLITT, J., and W. J. BATE. "The Distinctions Between Fancy and Imagination in Eighteenth-Century English Criticism." *MLN,* 60(1945):8–15.

18 CHAPMAN, Gerald Wester. See 1.6.

19 CLARK, Robert T. "Herder, Cesarotti, and Vico." *SP,* 44(1947):645–71.

20 CRANE, Ronald S. "English Neoclassical Criticism: An Outline Sketch." *C&C,* pp. 372–88.

21 ———. "On Writing the History of English Criticism, 1650–1800." *UTQ,* 22(1953):366–91.

22 ———. "Suggestions Toward a Genealogy of 'The Man of Feeling.' " *ELH,* 1(1934):205–30.

1 CROCE, Benedetto. "Estetici italiani della seconda metà del settecento." In his *Problemi di estetica*. 4th ed. Bari: Laterza, 1948.

2 ———. "La Teoria dell'arte e la critica letteraria." See 25.6.

3 DANZIGER, Marlies K. "Heroic Villains in Eighteenth-Century Criticism." *CL*, 11:35–46.

4 DAVIDSON, Hugh M. *Audience, Words, and Art: Studies in Seventeenth-Century French Rhetoric*. Columbus: Ohio State U P, 1966.

5 ———. "Yet Another View of French Classicism." *BuR*, 13(1965):51–62.

6 DOLPH, Joseph M. "Taste in Eighteenth-Century English Rhetorical Theory." *DA*, 25(1964):31–64. (Ore).

7 DRAPER, John William. *Eighteenth Century English Aesthetics: A Bibliography*. Heidelberg: Winter, 1931.

8 DURHAM, Willard Higley. See 1.11.

9 EATON, J. W. "The Beginnings of German Literary Criticism." *MLN*, 53(1938):351–56.

10 ELLEDGE, Scott. "The Background and Development in English Criticism on the Theories of Generality and Particularity." *PMLA*, 62(1947):147–82.

11 ———. *ECCE*. See 1.12.

12 ———, and Donald SCHIER. *CM*. See 1.13.

13 ENRIGHT, Dennis, and Ernst de CHICHERA. See 1.14.

14 FÉNELON. *Lettre sur les occupations de l'Académie française*. Paris: Delagrave, 1868.

15 FISCH, M. H. "The Coleridges, Dr. Prati and Vico." *MP*, 41(1943–4):111–12.

16 FOERSTER, Donald M. *Homer in English Criticism: The Historical Approach of the Eighteenth Century*. New Haven: Yale U P, 1947. [YSE, 105.]

17 FUBINI, Mario, and Ettore BONORA, eds. *Antologia della critica letteraria*, III. *Dall'Arcadia agli inizi del Novecento*. 7th ed. enl. Turin: Petrini, 1961.

18 GEBERT, Clara. See 1.16.

19 GILLOT, Hubert. *La Querelle des anciens et des modernes en France*. Paris, 1914.*

20 GOLENIŠČIV-KUTUZOV, I. "Barokko, klassicizm, romantizm (Literaturnye teorii Itallii XVII–XIX vekov)." *VLit*, 8(1964):104–26.

21 GRAHAM, H. G. *Scottish Men of Letters in the Eighteenth Century*. New York: Macmillan, 1901.

22 GREEN, Clarence Corleon. "Poetic Justice." In his *The Neoclassic Theory of Tragedy in England During the Eighteenth Century*. Cambridge, Mass.: Harvard U P, 1934.

1 GUSTAFSSON, Lars. " 'Imitation' och 'entusiasm': En studie i klassicistick poetik." *Samlaren*, 74(1963):144–75.

2 HAASE, Erich. "Zur Bedeutung von 'je ne sais quoi' im 17. Jahrhundert." *ZFSL*, 67(1956):47–68.

3 HAINES, Charles Moline. *Shakespeare in France: Criticism: Voltaire to Victor Hugo.* London: Milford, Oxford U P, 1925.

4 HALE, Paul Vincent. " 'Enthusiasm' Rejected and Espoused in English Poetry and Criticism, 1660–1740." *DA*, 24:727 (NYU).

5 HANZO, T. H. *Latitude and Restoration Criticism.* Copenhagen: Rosenkilde and Bagger, 1961. [Anglistica, 12.] [Humanities]

6 HATFIELD, Henry. *Aesthetic Paganism in German Literature: From Winckelmann to the Death of Goethe.* Cambridge, Mass.: Harvard U P, 1964.

7 HATHAWAY, Baxter. "The Lucretian 'Return upon Ourselves' in Eighteenth-Century Theories of Tragedy." *PMLA*, 62(1947):672–89.

8 HAVENS, George R. "Pre-Romanticism in France." *ECr*, 6(1966):63–76.

9 HAVENS, R. D. "Changing Taste in the Eighteenth Century." *PMLA*, 44(1929):501–36.

10 HEIDLER, Joseph B. *The History, from 1700 to 1800, of English Criticism of Prose Fiction.* Urbana: U of Illinois P, 1928. [ISLL, 13, 2.]

11 HILDEBRANDT-GÜNTHER, Renate. *Antike Rhetorik und deutsche literarische Theorie im 17. Jahrhundert.* Marburg: Elwert, 1966.

12 HIPPLE, Walter John, Jr. *The Beautiful, the Sublime, and the Picturesque in Eighteenth-Century British Aesthetic Theory.* Carbondale: Southern Illinois U P, 1957.

13 HOOKER, Edward N. "The Discussion of Taste, from 1750 to 1770, and New Trends in Literary Criticism." *PMLA*, 49(1934):577–92.

14 ———. "Humour in the Age of Pope." *HLQ*, 11(1948):361–85.

15 HOWELL, A. C. "*Res et Verba:* Words and Things." *ELH*, 13(1946):131–42.

16 HUGHES, Richard E. " 'Wit': The Genealogy of a Theory." *CLA Journal*, 5(1961):142–44.

17 HYNES, Samuel. See 2.3.

18 JACKSON, Wallace. "Immediacy: The Development of a Critical Concept from Addison to Coleridge." *DA*, 25(1964):3574–75 (Penn).

19 JOHNSON, Maurice O. *The Sin of Wit.* Syracuse: Syracuse U P, 1950.

20 JONAS, Leah. *The Divine Science: The Aesthetic of Some Representative Seventeenth-Century English Poets.* New York: Columbia U P, 1940.

21 JONES, Edmund David. See 2.4.

1 JONES, R. F. "Science and Criticism in the Neo-Classical Age of English Literature." *JHI*, 1:381–412.

2 KALLICH, Martin. "The Association of Ideas and Critical Theory: Hobbes, Locke and Addison." *ELH*, 12(1945):290–315.

3 ———. "The Associationist Criticism of Francis Hutcheson and David Hume." *SP*, 43(1946):644–67.

4 KEESEY, Donald Earl. "Dramatic Criticism in the *Gentleman's Magazine*, 1731–1754." *SB*, 18:81–109.

5 KENION, Alonzo Williams. "The Influence of Criticism upon English Tragedy, 1700–1750." *DA*, 24:298–99 (Duke).

6 KERN, Edith. *The Influence of Heinsius and Vossius upon French Dramatic Theory*. Baltimore: Johns Hopkins P, 1949.

7 KINGHORN, A. M. "Literary Aesthetics and the Sympathetic Emotions— A Main Trend in Eighteenth-Century Scottish Criticism." *SSL*, 1(1963):35–47.

8 KLAVER, Peter Roberts. "The Meaning of the Term 'Wit' in English Literary Criticism: 1680–1712." *DA*, 27(1966):478A–9A (Mich).

9 KNIGHT, Dorothy. "The Development of the Imagery of Colour in German Literary Criticism from Gottsched to Herder." *MLR*, 56(1961):354–72.

10 KRAPP, Robert M. "Class Analysis of a Literary Controversy: Wit and Sense in Seventeenth-Century English Literature." *Science and Society*, 10(1946):80–92.

11 KRAUSS, Werner, and Hans KORTUM. See 2.6.

12 KRISTELLER, Paul O. "The Modern System of the Arts: A Study in the History of Aesthetics." *JHI*, 12(1951):496–527; 13(1952):17–46.

13 KULAS, James Edward. "Comic Characters in Eighteenth-Century English Fiction: A View of the Theory, Types and Techniques." *DA*, 23:3353–54 (Wis).

14 KURAK, Alex. "Imitation, Burlesque Poetry and Parody: A Study of Some Augustan Critical Distinctions." *DA*, 24(1963):2014–15 (Minn).

15 LA HARPE, Jean-François. *Lycée, ou cours de littérature ancienne et moderne*. 2 vols. Paris: Didier, 1834.

16 LEGOUIS, Pierre. "Corneille and Dryden as Dramatic Critics." *Seventeenth Century Studies Presented to Sir Herbert Grierson*. New York: Octagon 1967, pp. 269–78. [Reprint of 1938 edition.]

17 LEITH, J. A. *The Idea of Art as Propaganda in France, 1750–1799*. Toronto: U of Toronto P, 1965.

18 LIPKING, Lawrence Irwin. "The Ordering of the Arts: Modes of Systematic Discourse in Eighteenth-Century English Histories and Criticism of Painting, Music and Poetry." *DA*, 24:729–30 (Cornell).

19 LOFTIS, John. See 2.7.

1　LOVEJOY, A. O. " 'Nature' as Aesthetic Norm." *MLN*, 42(1927):444–50.

2　——. "The Parallelism of Deism and Classicism." *MP*, 29(1932):281–99.

3　McCOSH, James. *The Scottish Philosophy, Biographical, Expository, Critical, from Hutcheson to Hamilton.* London: Macmillan, 1875.

4　McCUTCHEON, Roger P. "Eighteenth Century Aesthetics: A Search for Surviving Values." *HLB*, 10:287–305.

5　McDONALD, Charles O. "Restoration Comedy as Drama of Satire: An Investigation into Seventeenth Century Aesthetics." *SP*, 61(1964):522–44.

6　MACLEAN, Norman. "From Action to Image: Theories of the Lyric in the Eighteenth Century." *C&C*, pp. 408–60.

7　MANN, Elizabeth L. "The Problem of Originality in English Literary Criticism, 1750–1800." *PQ*, 18(1939):97–118.

8　MANWARING, Elizabeth W. *Italian Landscape in Eighteenth-Century England.* New York: Oxford U P, 1925.

9　MARKS, Emerson R. *Relativist and Absolutist: The Early Neoclassical Debate in England.* New Brunswick, N.J.: Rutgers U P, 1955.

10　MARTIN, Albert T. " 'Paper-Geniuses' of the Anglican Pulpit." *QJS*, 51:286–93.

11　MAUROCORDATO, Alexandre. "La Critique classique anglaise et la fonction de la tragédie (1600–1720)." *EA*, 14:10–24.

12　——. *La Critique classique en Angleterre de la Restoration à la mort de Joseph Addison: Essai de définition.* Paris: Didier, 1964. [EA, 18]

13　MAZZEO, Joseph A. "Metaphysical Poetry and the Poetic of Correspondence." *JHI*, 14:221–34.

14　——. "A Seventeenth-Century Theory of Metaphysical Poetry." *RR*, 42(1951):245–53.

15　MELCHIONDA, Mario. "Davenant, Hobbes, Sprat: Introduzione alla critica letteraria della Restaurazione." *FeL*, 11(1965):317–36:416–48.

16　MONK, Samuel Holt. "Grace Beyond the Reach of Art." *JHI*, 5(1944):131–50.

17　——. *The Sublime: Study of Critical Theories in Eighteenth-Century England.* Ann Arbor: U of Michigan P, 1960. [AA40]*†

18　MYERS, Robert M. "Neo-Classical Criticism of the *Ode for Music*." *PMLA*, 62(1947):399–421.

19　NEEDHAM, H. A. *Taste and Criticism in the Eighteenth Century.* London: Harrap, 1952.

20　NELSON, Robert J. "Modern Criticism of French Classicism: Dimensions of Definition." *BuR*, 13(1965):37–50.

1 NEWMAN, Robert Stanley. "The Tragedy of Wit: The Development of Heroic Drama from Dryden to Addison." *DA*, 25(1964):5262 (UCLA).

2 NITCHIE, Elizabeth. "Longinus and the Theory of Poetic Imitation in Seventeenth and Eighteenth Century England." *SP*, 32(1935):580–97.

3 OGDEN, H. V. S. "The Principles of Variety and Contrast in Seventeenth Century Aesthetics and Milton's Poetry." *JHI*, 10(1949):159–82.

4 ONG, Walter J. "Psyche and the Geometers: Aspects of Associationist Critical Theory." *MP*, 49(1951):16–27.

5 PAPAJEWSKI, Helmut. "Die Bedeutung der *Ars Poetica* für den englischen Neoklassizismus." *Anglia*, 79(1961):406–39.

6 PETRONIO, Guiseppe. See 2.9.

7 PEYRE, Henri. *Le Classicisme français*. New York: Maison Française, 1942.

8 ———. *Qu'est-ce que le classicisme?* Rev. and enl. ed. Paris: Nizet, 1965.

9 PHILLIPS, James E. "Poetry and Music in the Seventeenth Century." In his *Music and Literature in England in the Seventeenth and Eighteenth Centuries*. Los Angeles: Clark Memorial Library, U.C.L.A., 1953.

10 PINTARD, René. "1600: La Littérature et le goût au seuil de l'époque 'classique.' " *DSS*, 50–51:5–7.

11 PURPUS, Eugene R. "The 'Plain, Easy and Familiar Way': The Dialogue in English Literature 1600–1725." *ELH*, 17(1950):47–58.

12 QUIGLEY, Hugh. *Italy and the Rise of a New School of Criticism in the Eighteenth Century*. Perth: Munro & Scott, 1921.

13 RAGSDALE, J. Donald. "Invention in English 'Stylistic' Rhetorics: 1600–1800." *QJS*, 51:164–67.

14 RIGAULT, E. *Historie de la querelle des anciens et des modernes*. New York: Franklin, 1963.

15 ROBERTSON, John G. *Studies in the Genesis of Romantic Theory in the Eighteenth Century*. New York: Russell & Russell, 1962.*

16 RØSTVIG, Maren-Sofie. *The Background of English Neoclassicism: With Some Comments on Swift and Pope*. Oslo: Universitetsforl, 1961

17 ROTHSTEIN, Eric. "English Tragic Theory in the Late Seventeenth Century." *ELH*, 29(1962):306–23.

18 SACKETT, Samuel John. *English Literary Criticism, 1726–1750*. Hays: Fort Hays Kansas State Col, 1962. [Fort Hays Studies, n.s. Literature Series, 1.]

19 SAINT-VICTOR, Pierre M. de. "Les Théories littéraires de l'Encyclopédie." *DA*, 26(1965):1019–20 (Ind).

20 SAISSELIN, Rémy G. "Some Remarks on French Eighteenth-Century Writing on the Arts." *JAAC*, 25(1966):187–96.

1 SAULNIER, Verdun L. *La Littérature française du siècle classique, 1610–1715.* 2nd ed. rev. Paris: P U de France, 1947.

2 ———. *La Littérature française du siècle philosophique.* 7th ed. rev. Paris: P U de France, 1963.

3 SCHUELLER, Herbert M. "Correspondences Between Music and the Sister Arts, According to Eighteenth-Century Aesthetic Theory." *JAAC*, 11:334–59.

4 ———. "'Imitation' and 'Expression' in British Music Criticism in the Eighteenth Century." *Musical Quarterly*, 34(1948):544–66.

5 ———. "Literature and Music as Sister Arts: An Aspect of Aesthetic Theory in Eighteenth-Century Britain." *PQ*, 26(1947):193–205.

6 ———. "The Use and Decorum of Music as Described in British Literature, 1700–1780," *JHI*, 13(1952):73–93.

7 SELLSTROM, A. Donald. "Rhetoric and the Poetics of French Classicism." *FR*, 34(1961):425–31.

8 SHUGRUE, Michael. "Applebee's Original Weekly Journal: An Index to Eighteenth-Century Taste." *NLB*, 6(1964):108–21.

9 SIMON, Irène. "Critical Terms in Restoration Translations from the French." *RBPH*, 42(1964):852–79; 43(1965):902–26.

10 SINGH, Sarup. *The Theory of Drama in the Restoration Period.* Bombay: Orient Longmans, 1963.

11 SMITH, David Nichol. See 2.12.

12 ———. *Shakespeare in the Eighteenth Century.* Oxford: Clarendon P, 1928.

13 SMITH, George Gregory. See 2.13.

14 SMITH, L. P. *Four Words: Romantic, Originality, Creative, Genius.* Oxford: Clarendon P, 1924.*

15 SPINGARN, Joel Elias. See 2.15.

16 STEWART, John Keith. "The Ballad in Relation to Eighteenth-Century Critical Theory." *DA*, 22(1961):862 (Princeton).

17 STOLL, E. E. "Oedipus and Othello: Corneille, Rymer and Voltaire." *Revue anglo-americaine*, 12(1934–34):385–400.

18 SWAIN, Victor Crowell. "On the Meaning of 'Wit' in Seventeenth-Century England." *DA*, 22:3189–90 (Colum).

19 SWEDENBERG, H. T., Jr. "Rules and English Critics of the Epic, 1650–1800." *SP*, 35(1938):566–87.

20 ———. *The Theory of the Epic in England, 1650–1800.* Berkeley: U of California P, 1944.

21 TAVE, Stuart M. *The Amiable Humorist: A Study in the Comic Theory and Criticism of the Eighteenth and Early Nineteenth Centuries.* Chicago: U of Chicago P, 1960.

22 TAYLER, Edmund William. See 2.16.

23 TAYLOR, Houghton W. "'Particular Character': An Early Phase of a Literary Evolution." *PMLA*, 60(1945):161–74.

1 TONNELAT, E. "Lessing et Corneille: Interprêtes d'Aristote." *Revue des cours et conferences*, 33:72–4.

2 TUVE, Rosamond. *Elizabethan and Metaphysical Imagery*. Chicago: U of Chicago P, 1967. [Pheonix-P68.]†

3 ———. "Imagery and Logic: Ramus and Metaphysical Poetics." *JHI*, 3(1942):365–400.

4 USTICK, W. L., and H. H. HUDSON. "Wit, 'Mixt Wit,' and the Bee in Amber." *HLB*, 8(1935):103–30.

5 VAN TIEGHEM, Paul. *L'Année littéraire (1754–1790)*. Geneva: Slatkine, 1966.

6 WADDINGTON, Raymond Bruce, Jr. "The Aesthetics of Some Seventeenth-Century Platonic Poets." *DA*, 26(1965):3310 (Rice).

7 WALTON, Geoffrey. "Seventeenth-Century Ideas of Wit." In his *Metaphysical to Augustan*. London: Bowes and Bowes, 1955.

8 WASSERMAN, Earl. "The Inherent Values of Eighteenth-Century Personification." *PMLA*, 65(1950):435–63.

9 ———. "The Pleasures of Tragedy." *ELH*, 14(1947):283–307.

10 WELLEK, René. *History of Modern Criticism, 1750–1950*. I: *The Later Eighteenth Century*. New Haven: Yale U P, 1955.*

11 ———. "The Term and Concept of 'Classicism' in Literary History." In *Aspects of the Eighteenth Century*, ed. Earl R. Wasserman. Baltimore: Johns Hopkins P, 1965, pp. 105–28.*

12 WHITNEY, Lois. *Primitivism and the Idea of Progress in English Popular Literature of the Eighteenth Century*. Baltimore: Johns Hopkins P, 1934.

13 WILLIAMSON, George. "The Restoration Revolt Against Enthusiasm." *SP*, 30(1933):571–603.

14 ———. "The Rhetorical Pattern of Neo-Classical Wit." *MP*, 33(1935):55–82.

15 WOOD, Paul Spencer. "The Opposition to Neo-Classicism in England Between 1660 and 1700." *MLA*, 43(1928):182–97.

16 WOOD, Theodore Edmundson Brown. "The Word 'Sublime' and Its Context, 1650–1760." *DA*, 26(1966):5421 (Penn).

17 WRIGHT, Charles Henry Conrad. *French Classicism*. Cambridge, Mass.: Harvard U P, 1920.

Individual Authors

Joseph Addison

18 *Addison: Criticism on Paradise Lost*, ed. Albert S. Cook. New York, 1926.

19 *Critique on "Paradise Lost"* . . . with remarks on the versification of Milton by Samuel Johnson . . . . London: Sharpe, 1805.

20 "An Essay on Virgil's *Georgics*." *ECCE*, 1:1–8. [1697.]

1 *The Lucubrations of Isaac Bickerstaff, Esq.* [*The Tatler.*] 4 vols. London, 1710–11.

2 *The Spectator by Addison and Steele and Others,* ed. George Gregory Smith. 4 vols. New York: Dutton, 1958. [1897–98.] [For literary criticism see especially Nos. 40, 62, 70, 74, 160, 249, 253, 297, 409, 411–21, 592.]

3 ——— and Richard Steele. *The Tatler,* ed. Lewis Gibbs. New York: Dutton, 1953. [Everyman's Library, No. 993.] [For literary criticism see especially No. 165].

4 *The Works of the Late Right Honourable Joseph Addison,* "including the whole contents of Bp. Hurd's edition, with letters and other pieces not found in any previous collection," ed. G. W. Greene. 6 vols. New York: Putnam, 1856.

*   *   *

5 BROADUS, E. K. "Joseph Addison as a Literary Critic." *University Magazine.* Montreal, 1909.

6 ELIOSEFF, Lee Andrew. *The Cultural Milieu of Addison's Literary Criticism.* Austin: U of Texas P, 1963.

7 MAHONEY, John L. "Addison and Akenside: The Impact of Psychological Criticism on Early English Romantic Poetry." *BJA,* 6:365–74.*

8 MORRIS, Robert L. "Addison's *Mixt Wit.*" *MLN,* 57(1942):666–68.

9 NEUMANN, Joshua H. "Shakespearean Criticism in *The Tatler* and *The Spectator.*" *PMLA,* 34(1924):612–23.

10 THORPE, Clarence D. "Addison and Hutcheson on the Imagination." *ELH,* 2(1925):222–29.

11 ———. "Addison and Some of His Predecessors on 'Novelty.'" *PMLA,* 52(1937):1114–29.

12 ———. "Addison's Contribution to Criticism." In *The Seventeenth Century,* ed. R. F. Jones. Stanford: Stanford U P, 1951, pp. 316–29.

13 ———. "Addison's Theory of the Imagination as 'Perceptive Response.'" *Michigan Academy of Science, Arts, and Letters,* 21(1936):509–30.

14 WILKINSON, Jean. "Some Aspects of Addison's Philosophy of Art." *HLQ,* 28(1964):31–44.

Mark Akenside

15 *The Pleasures of Imagination.* London: Dodsley, 1744.

*   *   *

16 MAHONEY, John L. See 61.7.

Vittorio Alfieri

17 *Del principe e delle lettere,* ed. Luigi Russo. Florence: F. de Monnier, 1943.

*   *   *

62

VITTORIO ALFIERI

1   MASIELLO, Vittorio. *L'Ideologia tragica di Vittorio Alfieri*. Rome: Ateneo, 1964.

2   SCRIVANO, Riccardo. "L'Alfieri critico di se stesso." *RLI*, 67(1962):259–72.

Archibald Alison

3   *Essays on the Nature and Principles of Taste*. London: Robinson, 1790.

4   *Essays on the Nature and Principles of Taste by A. Alison*. Repr. of 5th ed. London, 1879.

*   *   *

5   KALLICH, Martin. "The Meaning of Archibald Alison's *Essays on Taste*." *PQ*, 27(1948):314–24.

6   STOLNITZ, Jerome. " 'Beauty': Some Stages in the History of an Idea." *JHI*, 22(1961): 185–204.

7   ——. "On the Origins of 'Aesthetic Disinterestedness.' " *JAAC*, 20(1961): 131–43.

Abbé d'Aubignac

8   [François Hédelin.] *Practique du théâtre*, ed. Pierre Martino. Algiers: Bastide-Jourdan, 1927. [1657.]

9   "Selections from *The Whole Art of the Stage*," trans. anon. *CM*, pp. 96–116. [1657.]

*   *   *

10 KNUTSON, Harold C. "D'Aubignac's Blind Spot: Comedy." *NM*, 67(1965):125–31.

Giuseppe Baretti

11 [Giuseppe Marco Antonio Baretti.] *A Dissertation upon Italian Poetry in Which Are Interspersed Some Remarks on Mr. Voltaire's Essay on the Epic Poets*. London: Dodsley, 1753.

12 *La Frusta letteraria*, ed. Luigi Piccioni. 2 vols. Bari: Laterza, 1932. [1763–65.]

13 *Prefazioni e polemiche*, ed. Luigi Piccioni. Bari: Laterza, 1911.

*   *   *

14 CROCE, Benedetto. "G. Baretti." In his *Problemi di estetica e contributi alla storia della estetica italiano*. Bari: Laterza, 1909, pp. 443–48.

15 DEUALLE, Albertina. *Giuseppe Baretti, suoi rapporti con Voltaire, Johnson e Parini*. Milan: Hoepli, 1932.

Abbé Charles Batteux

16 *Les Beaux-Arts réduits à un mème principe*. Paris: Durand, 1746.

17 *A Course of the Belles Lettres: Or the Principles of Literature*, trans. M. Miller. 4 vols. London: Low, 1761.

Alexander Gottlieb Baumgarten

1 *Aesthetica.* 2 vols in 1. Hildesheim: Olms, 1961. [Repr. of 1750 ed., Frankfurt.]

2 *Reflections on Poetry: Alexander Gottlieb Baumgarten's Meditationes philosophicae de nonnullis ad poema pertinentibus*, trans. Karl Aschenbrenner and William B. Holther. Berkeley: U of California P, 1954. [1735.]

* * *

3 CROCE, Benedetto. "Rileggendo l'"Aesthetica' del Baumgarten." In his *Ultimi saggi.* Bari: Laterza, 1948.

4 RIEMANN, Albert. *Die Aesthetik A. G. Baumgartens.* Halle: Niemeyer, 1928.

James Beattie

5 *Dissertations Moral and Critical.* London: Strahen, 1783.

6 *Essays on Poetry and Music.* 3d ed. London, 1779.

7 "From *Dissertations Moral and Critical:* From 'On Fable and Romance.' " *ECCE*, 2:920–31. [1783.]

8 "From *Essays on Poetry and Music, as They Affect the Mind*: 'Of Sympathy.' " *ECCE*, 2:914–20. [1776.]

Cesare Beccaria

9 *Ricerche intorno alla natura dello stile.* Milan, 1770.

Giulio Cesare Becelli

10 *Della novella poesia, cioè del vero genere e particolari bellezze della poesia italiana.* Verona, 1732.

Saverio Bettinelli

11 *Lettere virgiliane. Lettere inglesi e Mia vita letteraria*, ed. Gilberto Finzi. Milan: Rizzoli, 1962. [1757.]

* * *

12 CROCE, Benedetto. "Le *Lettre Virgiliane* de Bettinelli" and "Bettinelli e Dante," in *Pagine Sparse.* Naples: Ricciardi, 1943, I, 421–27.

Sir Richard Blackmore

13 *Essay upon Wit*, ed. Richard C. Boys. Ann Arbor: U of Michigan Press, 1946. [1716.]

14 "Preface to *Prince Arthur.*" *CESC*, 3:227–41. [1695.]

15 *Satyr Against Wit.* London, 1700. [1699.]

* * *

1 BOYS, Richard C. *Sir Richard Blackmore and the Wits.* New York: Octagon, 1969.

2 DOUGLAS, Loyd. "A Severe Animadversion on Bossu." *PMLA*, 62(1947): 690–706.

3 KRAPP, Robert M. "Class Analysis of a Literary Controversy: Wit and Sense in Seventeenth-Century English Literature." *Science and Society*, 10(1946):80–92.

Thomas Blackwell

4 *Enquire into the Life and Writings of Homer.* 2nd ed. London, 1736. [1735.]

5 "From *An Inquiry into the Life and Writings of Homer.*" *ECCE*, 1:432–47.

* * *

6 WHITNEY, Lois. "English Primitivistic Theories of Epic Origins." *MP*, 21(1924):337–78.

7 ———. "Thomas Blackwell, a Disciple of Shaftesbury." *PQ*, 5(1926):196–211.

Hugh Blair

8 *Dissertation on the Poems of Ossian.* London: Becket, 1763.

9 "From *A Critical Dissertation on the Poems of Ossian, the Son of Fingal.*" *ECCE*, 2:848–59.

10 *Lectures on Rhetoric and Belles Lettres.* 6th ed. London: Strahan, Cadell, 1796. [1783.]

11 *Lectures on Rhetoric and Belles Lettres*, ed. Harold F. Harding. 2 vols. Carbondale: Southern Illinois U P, 1965. [Landmarks in Rhetoric and Public Address.]

Johann Jakob Bodmer

12 *Critische Abhandlung von dem Wunderbaren in der Poesie.* Zürich, 1740.

13 *Critische Betrachtungen über die poetischen Gemählde der Dichter.* Zürich, 1741.

14 *Von dem Einfluss und Gebrauche der Einbildungs-Kraft*, with J. J. Breitinger. Frankfurt and Leipzig, 1727.

* * *

15 RAZZANO, Annamaria. "Bodmer e Breitinger e l'estetica sei-settecentesca italiana." *RdE*, 8(1963):61–87.

Nicolas Boileau-Despreaux

1 *The Art of Poetry*, "written in French by the Sieur de Boileau. Made English by Sir William Soame; since revis'd by John Dryden, Esq." London, 1710. [1674.]

2 COOK, Albert S. See 1.7.

3 *L'Arte poétique de Boileau*, ed. Henri Bénac. Paris: Hachette, 1946.

4 *Oeuvres complètes*, ed. Françoise Escal. Paris: Gallimard, 1966.

5 *Les Réflexions sur Longin et pages choisies de toute son oeuvre à l'exclusion de l'art poétique choix et notices*, ed. M. Bonfanti and S. Zoppi. Turin: Giappichelli, 1965. [1693?]

6 *Selected Criticism*, trans. Ernest Dilworth. Indianapolis: Bobbs-Merrill, 1965. [LLA-218]†

*   *   *

7 ALBALAT, Antoine. *L'Art poétique de Boileau*. Paris: Société Française d'Éditions Littéraires et Techniques, 1929.

8 BONFANTI, Mario. *L'Art poétique de Boileau e i suoi problemi*. Milan: La Goliardica, 1957.

9 BRODY, Jules. *Boileau and Longinus*. Geneva: Droz, 1958.

10 CLARK, Alexander F. B. *Boileau and the French Classical Critics in England*. Paris: Champion, 1925.

11 DAVIDSON, Hugh M. "The Idea of Literary History in the *Art Poétique* of Boileau." *Symposium*, 18(1964):264–72.

12 ———. "The Literary Arts of Longinus and Boileau." In *Studies in Seventeenth-Century French Literature Presented to Morris Bishop*, ed. Jean-Jacques Demorest. Ithaca: Cornell U P, 1962, pp. 247–64.

13 EDELMAN, Nathan. "*L'Art poétique:* 'Long-temps plaire, et jamais ne lasser.'" In *Studies in Seventeenth-Century French Literature Presented to Morris Bishop*, ed. Jean-Jacques Demorest. Ithaca: Cornell U P, 1962, pp. 231–46.

Jacques Bénigne Bossuet

14 *Maximes et réflexions sur la comédie*. Paris: Jean Anisson, 1694.

*   *   *

15 CHRISTOFIDES, C. G. "Bossuet on Dramatic Theory." *Symposium*, 16(1962):225–27.

16 GOYET, Thérèse. "Antiquité et modernité chez Bossuet." *IL*, 18(1966):93–98.

17 REYNOLDS, Ernest E. *Bossuet*. New York: Doubleday, 1963.

James Boswell

1 *Boswell's Life of Johnson, Together with Boswell's Journal of a Tour to the Hebrides and Johnson's Diary of a Journey into North Wales,* ed. George Birkbeck Hill. Rev. and enl. ed. by L. F. Powell. 2d ed. Oxford: Clarendon P, 1964–

2 *Life of Johnson.* London: Oxford U P, 1953. [Modern Library-T62]

*   *   *

3 GOLDEN, James L. "Boswell on Rhetoric and Belles-Lettres." *QJS*, 50:266–76.

4 LUSTIG, Irma S. "Boswell's Literary Criticism in The Life of Johnson." *SEL*, 6(1966):529–41.

Dominique Bouhours

5 *The Arts of Logick and Rhetorick*, trans. John Oldmixon. London, 1728. [1687.] [Translation of *La Manière.* . . .]

6 "The Bel Esprit from *The Conversations of Aristo and Eugene*," trans. Donald Schier. *CM*, pp. 206–27. [1671.]

7 *Entretiens d'Ariste et d'Eugène.* Last ed. Amsterdam: Jacques le Jeune, 1671.

8 *Entretiens d'Ariste et d'Eugène*, ed. René Radonant. Paris, 1920.

9 "The Je Ne Sais Quoi from *The Conversations of Aristo and Eugene*," trans. Donald Schier. *CM*, pp. 228–38.

10 *La Manière de bien penser dans les ouvrages de l'esprit.* Paris: La Veuve de Sebastien Mabre-Cramoisy, 1687.

11 "Selections from *The Art of Criticism*," trans. "A person of quality" (London, 1705). *CM*, pp. 239–74. [1687.]

Johann Jakob Breitinger

12 *Critische Dichtkunst*, ed. V. Wolfgang Bender. 2 vols. Stuttgart: Metzler, 1966. [Repr. of 1740 ed.]

Comte de Buffon

13 [Georges Louis Leclerc.] *Discours sur le style . . . avec une notice biographique . . . et des notes explicatives par A. Hatzfeld.* Paris, 1872.

14 *Oeuvres philosophiques*, ed. J. Piveteau, M. Fréchet, and C. Bruneau. 1st ed. Paris: P U de France, 1954. [For literary criticism see especially the section entitled "Buffon Écrivain."]

Edmund Burke

1 *A Philosophical Inquiry into the Origin of Our Ideas of the Sublime and Beautiful.* London: Routledge and Kegan Paul, 1958. [1757.]

2 *The Philosophy of Edmund Burke: A Selection from His Speeches and Writings*, ed. Louis I. Bredvold and Ralph G. Ross. Ann Arbor: U of Michigan P, 1960. [AA121.]†

3 *Selected Writings of Edmund Burke*, ed. Walter J. Bate. New York: Modern Library, 1960.

*   *   *

4 COBBAN, Alfred. *Edmund Burke and the Revolt Against the Eighteenth Century.* London: Allen, 1929.*

5 ERHARDT-SIEBOLD, Erika von. "Harmony of the Senses in English, German, and French Romanticism." *PMLA*, 48(1932):577–92.

6 HOWARD, William G. "Burke Among the Forerunners of Lessing." *PMLA*, 22(1907):608–32.

7 MOORE, T. M. *The Backgrounds of Burke's Theory of the Sublime, 1660–1759.* Ithaca: Cornell U P, 1933.

8 STAVER, Frederick Lee. "Edmund Burke's Theory of the Sublime and Its Background." *DA*, 24:5391 (Calif).

9 WECTER, Dixon. "Burke's Theory Concerning Words, Images, and Emotion." *PMLA*, 55(1940):167–81.

10 WESTON, John C., Jr. "Edmund Burke's Wit." *REL*, 4(1963):95–107.

11 WICHELNS, Herbert A. "Burke's *Essay on the Sublime* and Its Reviewers." *JEGP*, 21(1922):645–61.

12 WOOD, Neal. "The Aesthetic Dimension of Burke's Political Thought." *JBS*, 4(1964):41–64.

Edward Bysshe

13 *The Art of English Poetry.* London: Kraplock, 1702. [1701.]

14 *The Art of English Poetry, 1708.* Los Angeles: Clark Memorial Library, U of California, 1953. [ARS, 40.]

Pietro Calepio

15 [Pietro dei Conti di Calepio.] *Paragone della poesia tragica d'Italia con quella di Francia.* Zurich, 1732.

George Campbell

16 *The Philosophy of Rhetoric.* London: Strahan, 1776.

17 *The Philosophy of Rhetoric*, ed. Lloyd F. Bitzer. Carbondale: Southern Illinois U P, 1963. [Landmarks in Rhetoric and Public Address.]

*   *   *

1 BITZER, Lloyd Frank. "The Lively Idea: A Study of Hume's Influence on George Campbell's *Philosophy of Rhetoric*." *DA*, 23(1962):351 (Iowa).

Melchiorre Cesarotti

2 *Saggi sulla filosofia delle lingue e del gusto di Melchior Cesarotti; si aggiunge: Il ragionamento sopra il diletto della tragedia.* Milan: Società Tipographia dei Classici Italiani, 1820. [1762.]

Jean Chapelain

3 *De la lecture des vieux romans.* 1st ed with notes by Alphonse Feillet. Paris: Aubry, 1870.

4 "His Opinion of the Poem *Adone*," trans. Donald Schier. *CM*, pp. 3–30. [1623.]

5 *Lettres*, ed. Tamizey de Larroque. 2 vols. Paris, 1880–83.

6 "On the Reading of the Old Romances," trans. Donald Schier. *CM*, pp. 31–54. [c. 1646.]

7 *Opuscules critiques.* Paris: Droz, 1936. [Société des Textes Français Modernes.]

8 *Les Sentimens de l'Académie française sur la tragi-comédie du Cid.* Paris: Camusat, 1638.

9 *Sentiments de l'Académie française sur le Cid*, ed. C. Searles. Minneapolis, 1916. [University of Minnesota Studies in Language and Literature, 3.]

Samuel Cobb

10 *Discourse on Criticism and of Poetry from "Poems on Several Occasions."* Ann Arbor: ARS, 1946. [1707.]

William Congreve

11 "Concerning Humour in Comedy." *CESC*, 3:242–52. [1695.]

12 "A Discourse on the Pindaric Ode." *ECCE*, 1:143–47. [1706.]

13 *An Essay Concerning Humor in Comedy.* Ann Arbor: ARS, 1947. [Ser. 1, no. 4. A facsim. of the ed. of 1744.]

14 *Letters upon Several Occasions*, ed. John Dennis. London, 1696.

15 *The Mourning Bride, Poems, & Miscellanies*, ed. Bonamy Dobrée. London: Milford, Oxford U P, 1928.

16 *William Congreve: Letters and Documents*, coll. and ed. John C. Hodges. London: Macmillan, 1964.

* * *

1 COSSE, Anthony Cabot. "Dramatic Theory and Practice in the Comedies of William Congreve." *DA*, 23(1962):1700–1701 (Colum).

Pierre Corneille

2 *Oeuvres complètes*, ed. André Stegmann. Paris: Seuil, 1963. [For literary criticism see especially "Discours de la tragédie et des moyens de la traiter selon le vraisemblable ou le nécessaire"; "Discours de l'utilité et des parties du poëme dramatique"; "Discours des trois unités d'action, de jour, et de lieu."]

3 *Trois discours sur le poème dramatique*, ed. Louis Forestier. Paris: C.D.U., 1964. [Text of 1660.]

4 *Writings on the Theatre*, ed. H. T. Barnwell. Oxford: Blackwell, 1965. [English and French.]

* * *

5 BARNWELL, H. T. "Some Reflexions on Corneille's Theory of 'Vraisemblance' as Formulated in the *Discours*." *FMLS*, 1(1965):295–310.

6 BRAY, René. *La Tragédie cornélienne devant la critique classique d'après la querelle de Sophonsibe*. Paris, 1927.

7 CHARLTON, D. G. "Corneille's Dramatic Theories and the 'Didacticism' of *Horace*." *FS*, 15(1961):1–11.

8 CROCE, Benedetto. *Ariosto, Shakespeare and Corneille*, trans. Douglas Ainslie. New York: Holt, 1920.

9 FISHER, Dorothea F. *Corneille and Racine in England*. New York: AMS Press, 1966. [Columbia Studies in Romance Philology and Literature, 5.]

10 LEEMAN, Richard Kendall. "Corneille and Dryden: Their Theories of Dramatic Poetry." *DA*, 22(1961):1158–59 (Wis).

11 LEMAÎTRE, Jules. *Corneille et la poétique d'Aristote*. Paris, 1888.

12 NELSON, Robert J. "The Spirit of Corneille's Criticism." *ECr*, 4(1964): 114–34.

13 SWEETSER, Marie Odile. *Les Conceptions dramatiques de Corneille d'après ses écrits théoriques*. Geneva: Droz; Paris: Minard, 1963.

Sir William Davenant

14 "Preface to *Gondibert*." *CESC*, 2:1–53. [1650.]

* * *

1 DOWLIN, Cornell March. *Sir William Davenant's Gondibert, Its Preface and Hobbe's Answer: A Study in English Neoclassicism.* Philadelphia, 1934.

2 HARBAGE, Alfred. *Sir William Davenant, Poet-Venturer, 1606–1668.* Philadelphia: U of Pennsylvania P, 1935.

3 MELCHIONDA, Mario. See 57.15.

4 NETHERCOT, Arthur Hobart. *Sir William D'Avenant, Poet Laureate and Playwright-Manager.* Chicago: U of Chicago P, 1938.

5 RENNER, Dick Arnold. "The Poetic Theory of Sir William Davenant in *Gondibert* and Its Preface." *DA*, 23:2519 (Mo).

John Dennis

6 "The Advancement and Reformation of Modern Poetry." In his *Miscellaneous Tracts.* London: The Author, 1727. [1701.]

7 *The Critical Works of John Dennis*, ed. Edward N. Hooker. 2 vols. Baltimore: Johns Hopkins P, 1939–43.

8 "The Grounds of Criticism in Poetry." *CEEC*, pp. 143–211. [1704.]

9 "The Impartial Critic." *CESC*, 3:148–97. [1693.]

10 "Reflections upon a Late Rhapsody Called *An Essay upon Criticism.*" *CEEC*, ed. W. H. Durham, pp. 212–53. [1711.]

11 *Remarks on Mr. Pope's "Rape of the Lock."* London: Roberts, 1728.

12 *Remarks upon Mr. Pope's Translation of Homer.* London, 1717.

* * *

13 HOOKER, Edward N. "Pope and Dennis." *ELH*, 7(1940):188–98.

14 RICHESON, Edward, Jr. "John Dennis as a Psychological Critic." *DA*, 23(1962):2118–19 (Bos).

René Descartes

15 BRUN, Jean. "Leibniz critique de Descartes." *RMM*, 67(1961):184–90.

16 KRANTZ, Émile. *L'Esthétique de Descartes, etudiée dans les rapports de la doctrine cartésienne avec la littérature classique française du XVIIième siècle.* Paris, 1882.

17 LEFÈVRE, Roger. *Le Criticisme de Descartes.* 1st ed. Paris: P U de France, 1958.

18 SHAPERE, Dudley. "Descartes and Plato." *JHI*, 24(1963):572–76.

Denis Diderot

1 *Diderot's Writings on the Theater*, ed. F. C. Green. Cambridge: U P, 1936. [French.]

2 *Oeuvres*, ed. André Billy. Paris: Gallimard, 1951. [Collection La Pléiade.]

3 *Oeuvres de théâtre ... avec un discours sur la poesie dramatique.* 2 vols. Paris: Duchesne & Delalain, 1771.

4 *Oeuvres esthétiques*, ed. Paul Vernière. Paris: Garnier, 1959.

* * *

5 BELAVAL, Yvon. *L'Esthétique sans paradoxe de Diderot*. Paris: Gallimard, 1950.

6 COMAILLE, Anne-Marie de. "Diderot et le symbole littéraire." In *Diderot Studies*, ed. Otis E. Fellows and Norman L. Torrey. Syracuse: Syracuse U P, 1950, pp. 94–120.

7 CROCKER, Lester G. *Two Diderot Studies: Ethics and Esthetics*. Baltimore: Johns Hopkins P, 1952.

8 CURTIUS, Ernst Robert. *Europäische Literatur und lateinisches Mittelalter*. Bern: Francke, 1948. [*European Literature and the Latin Middle Ages*, trans. W. R. Trask. London: Routledge and Kegan Paul, 1953.]* [See especially "Diderot und Horaz."]

9 DIECKMANN, Herbert. "Diderot's Conception of Genius." *JHI*, 2(1941): 151–82.

10 ———. "Zur Interpretation Diderots." *RF*, 53(1939):47–82.

11 FOLKIERSKI, Wladyslw. *Entre le classicisme et le romantisme*. Krakow: Polish Academy of Sciences and Letters, 1925.* [See especially pp. 355–516.]

12 GILLOT, Hubert. *Denis Diderot: L'Homme—ses idées philosophiques, esthétiques, littéraires*. Paris: Courville, 1937.

13 GILMAN, Margaret. "The Poet According to Diderot." *RR*, 37(1946):37–54.

14 KRAKEUR, L. G. "Aspects of Diderot's Aesthetic Theory." *RR*, 30(1939): 244–59.

15 MAY, Gita. "In Defense of Diderot's Art Criticism." *FR*, 37(1963):11–21.

16 MAYOUX, J. J. "Diderot and the Technique of Modern Literature." *MLR*, 31(1936):518–31.

17 MØLBERG, Hans. *Aspects de l'esthétique de Diderot*. Copenhagen: Schultz, 1964.

18 NIKLAUS, Robert. "La Portée des théories dramatiques de Diderot et de ses réalizations théâtrales." *RR*, 54(1963):6–19.

19 SAISSELIN, R. G. "Diderot as Art Critic." *FR*, 37(1964):457–60.

20 SPITZER, Leo. "The Style of Diderot." In his *Linguistics and Literary History: Essays in Stylistics*. New York: Russell & Russell, 1962.

1 STEEL, Eric M. "Diderot's Theory of Imagery." In his *Diderot's Imagery*. New York: Corporate P, 1947.

2 TOPAZIO, Virgil W. "Diderot's Limitations as an Art Critic." *FR*, 37(1963): 3–11.

3 VEXLER, Felix. *Studies in Diderot's Esthetic Naturalism.* New York, 1922.

4 WALKER, Eleanor M. "Towards an Understanding of Diderot's Esthetic Theory." *RR*, 35(1944):277–87.

Sir Kenelm Digby

5 *Treatise Declaring the Nature and Operations of Man's Soul: Out of which the Immortality of Reasonable Souls is Convinced.* London: Williams, 1657

John Dryden

6 *The Critical Opinions of John Dryden: A Dictionary*, ed. John M. Aden. Nashville: Vanderbilt U P, 1963.

7 *Dramatic Essays.* New York: Dutton, 1931. [Everyman's Library.]

8 *An Essay of Dramatic Poesy.* 2d ed. rev. London, 1684.

9 *An Essay of Dramatic Poesy. A Defense of an Essay of Dramatic Poesy. Preface to the Fables*, ed. John L. Mahoney. Indianapolis: Bobbs-Merrill, 1965. [LLA104]†

10 "Essay of Heroic Plays." Prefixed to his two-part heroic play *The Conquest of Granada*. London: T.N. for Henry Herringman, 1672.

11 *The Essays of John Dryden*, ed. W. P. Ker. 2 vols. Oxford: Clarendon P, 1926.

12 *Of Dramatic Poesy, and Other Critical Essays*, ed. George Watson. New York: Dutton, 1962. [Everyman's Library.]

13 "Preface to *Fables Ancient and Modern*." *ELC*, pp. 63–85. [1700.]

* * *

14 ARCHER, Stanley. "The Persons in *An Essay of Dramatic Poesy*." *PLL*, 2(1966):305–14.

15 ARUNDELL, Dennis Drew, ed. *Dryden and Howard, 1664–1668.* Cambridge: U P, 1929.

16 BREDVOLD, Louis I. *The Intellectual Milieu of John Dryden.* Ann Arbor: U of Michigan P, 1934. [AA3]*†

17 BROWER, Reuben A. "An Allusion to Europe: Dryden and Tradition." *ELH*, 19(1952):38–48.

18 ———. "Dryden and the 'Invention' of Pope." In *Restoration and Eighteenth-Century Literature in Honor of Alan Dugald McKillop*. Chicago: U of Chicago P, 1964, pp. 211–33. [Rice University Semicentennial Publications.]

1   EIDSON, John Olin. "Dryden's Criticism of Shakespeare." *SP*, 33(1936): 273–80.

2   ELIOT, T. S. *John Dryden: The Poet, the Dramatist, the Critic*. New York: Holliday, 1932.

3   ELLIS, Amanda M. "Horace's Influence on Dryden." *PQ*, 4(1925):39–60.

4   EMPSON, William. " 'Wit' in the *Essay on Criticism*." *HudR*, 2(1950):559–77.

5   FREEDMAN, Morris. "Milton and Dryden on Rhyme." *HLQ*, 24:337–44.

6   FRYE, Prosser Hall. "Dryden and the Critical Canons of the Eighteenth Century." *Nebraska University Studies*, 7(1907):1–39.

7   GATTO, Louis C. "An Annotated Bibliography of Critical Thought Concerning Dryden's *Essay of Dramatic Poesy*." *RECTR*, 5(1966):18–29.

8   HATHAWAY, Baxter. "John Dryden and the Function of Tragedy." *PMLA*, 58(1943):665–73.

9   HUNTLEY, Frank L. "Dryden's Discovery of Boileau." *MP*, 65(1947): 112–17.

10 ———. *On Dryden's "Essay of Dramatic Poesy."* Ann Arbor: U of Michigan P, 1951.

11 ———. "On the Persons of Dryden's *Essay of Dramatic Poesy*." *MLN*, 63(1948):88–95.

12 JONES, Richard Foster. *Ancients and Moderns: A Study of the Background of the "Battle of the Books."* St. Louis, 1936. [Washington University Studies, n.s. Language and Literature, 6.]

13 KAPLAN, Charles. "Dryden's *An Essay of Dramatic Poesy*." *Expl*, 8(1950): item 36.

14 KIRSCH, Arthur C. "Dryden's Theory and Practice of the Rhymed Heroic Play." *DA*, 22(1961):1979 (Princeton).

15 ———. "An Essay on *Dramatick Poetry* (1681)." *HLQ*, 28(1964):89–91.

16 LEEMAN, Richard Kendall. See 69.10.

17 MACE, Dean T. "Dryden's Dialogue on Drama." *JWCI*, 25(1962):87–112.

18 MONK, Samuel H. "Dryden and the Beginnings of Shakespeare Criticism in the Augustan Age." In *The Persistence of Shakespeare Idolatry: Essays in Honor of Robert W. Babcock*, ed. Herbert M. Schueller. Detroit: Wayne State U P, 1964, pp. 47–75.

19 MOORE, Frank Harper. *The Nobler Pleasure: Dryden's Comedy in Theory and Practice*. Chapel Hill: U of North Carolina P, 1963.

20 NOYES, G. R. "Crites in Dryden's *Essay of Dramatic Poesy*." *MLN*, 38(1923):333–37.

21 PENDLEBURY, Bevis John. *Dryden's Heroic Plays: A Study of the Origins*. London: Selwyn & Blount, 1923.

1 SIMON, Irène. "Dryden's Revision of the *Essay of Dramatic Poesy*." *RES*, 14(1963):132–41.

2 SINGH, Sarup. "Dryden and the Unities." *IJES*, 2(1961):78–90.

3 SMITH, David Nichol. *John Dryden*. Cambridge: U P, 1950.

4 SMITH, John H. "Dryden's Critical Temper." *Washington University Studies, Humanistic Series*, 12(1925):201–20.

5 THALE, Mary. "Dryden's Critical Vocabulary: The Imitation of Nature." *PLL*, 2(1966):315–26.

6 ———. "Dryden's Dramatic Criticism: Polestar of the Ancients." *CL*, 18(1966):36–54.

7 TROWBRIDGE, Hoyt. "Dryden's *Essay on the Dramatic Poetry of the Last Age*." *PQ*, 22(1943):240–50.

8 ———. "The Place of the Rules in Dryden's Criticism." *MP*, 44(1946):84–96.

9 VERRAL, A. W. *Lectures on Dryden*. Cambridge: U P, 1914.

10 WATSON, George. "Dryden's First Answer to Rymer." *RES*, 14(1963):17–23.

11 WHITE, Harold O. "Dryden and Descartes." *TLS*, December 19, 1929:1081.

12 WILLIAMSON, George. "The Occasion of *An Essay of Dramatic Poesy*." *MP*, 44(1946):1–9.

Abbé Jean Baptiste Du Bos

13 *Réflexions critiques sur la poésie et sur la peinture*. New ed. rev. and corrected. Utrecht: Neaulma, 1732–36. [1719.]

* * *

14 CARAMASCHI, Enzo. "Arte e critica nella concezione dell'Abate Du Bos." *RLMC*, 12(1959):101–18; 13(1960):248–70.

George Farquhar

15 "Discourse upon Comedy." *CEEC*, pp. 257–86. [1702.]

Henry Fielding

16 *Complete Works*. New York: Barnes and Noble, 1967. [For literary criticism see especially the introductory chapters of *Tom Jones*, the Preface to *Joseph Andrews*, and "The Purpose of Letters."]

17 "Introductory Chapters from *Tom Jones*." *ELC*, pp. 207–36. [1749.]

18 "Preface to *Joseph Andrews*." *ELC*, pp. 200–206. [1742.]

* * *

1 BISSELL, Frederick Olds. *Fielding's Theory of the Novel.* Ithaca: Cornell U P, 1933.

2 GOLDBERG, Homer. "Comic Prose Epic or Comic Prose Romance: The Argument of the Preface to *Joseph Andrews.*" *PQ*, 43(1964):193–215.

3 THORNBURY, Ethel Margaret. *Henry Fielding's Theory of the Comic Prose Epic.* Madison, 1931. [University of Wisconsin Studies in Language and Literature, 30.]

4 VOORDE, Frans Pieter Van der. *Henry Fielding, Critic and Satirist.* The Hague: Westerbaan, 1931.

Bernard Fontenelle

5 [Bernard Le Bovier de Fontenelle.] "A Digression on the Ancients and Moderns," trans. Donald Schier. *CM*, pp. 358–70. [1688.]

6 *Oeuvres.* 12 vols. New ed. Paris: B. Brunet, 1758–64. [For literary criticism see especially "Digression sur les anciens et les modernes," "Réflexions sur la poëtique," "Sur la poësie en général."]

7 "Of Pastorals," trans. Peter Motteux (London, 1695). *CM*, pp. 339–57. [1688.]

*   *   *

8 DIECKMANN, Herbert. "Esthetic Theory and Criticism in the Enlightenment: Some Examples of Modern Trends." In *Introduction to Modernity: A Symposium on Eighteenth Century Thought*, ed. Robert Mollenauer. Austin: U of Texas P, 1965, pp. 63–105.

Juan Pablo Forner

9 *El Asno erudito.* Madrid: Supremo Consejo de Indias, 1782.

10 *El Asno erudito*, ed. Manuel Muñoz Cortés. Valencia: Castalia, 1948.

11 *Oración apologética por la España y su mérito literario.* Madrid: Imprenta Real, 1786.

Alexander Gerard

12 *An Essay on Genius.* London, 1774.

13 *Essay on Taste.* 3d ed. Edinburgh: J. Bell, 1780. [1759.]

14 *An Essay on Taste, Together with Observations Concerning the Imitative Nature of Poetry*, ed. Walter J. Hipple. Gainesville, Fla.: SF&R, 1963. [A facsim. reprod. of the 3d ed., 1780.]

*   *   *

15 CAUVEL, Martha Jane. "The Critic, 'Blest with a Poet's Fire': Alexander Gerard's Interpretation of Genius, Taste, and Aesthetic Criticism." *DA*, 23:4382 (Bryn Mawr).

16 GRENE, Marjorie. "Gerard's *Essay on Taste.*" *MP*, 41(1943):45–58.

Heinrich Wilhelm Gerstenberg

1 *Briefe über Merkwürdigkeiten der Litteratur*, ed. Alexander von Weilen. Stuttgart, 1890. [1766.] [Deutsche Litteraturdenkmale, 29, 30.]

Charles Gildon

2 *Complete Art of Poetry*. London, 1718.

3 "An Essay at a Vindication of the Love-Verses of Cowley and Waller." *CEEC*, pp. 3–13. [1694.]

4 "From *The Complete Art of Poetry*, Part II." *CEEC*, pp. 18–75. [1718.]

5 "Modern Poets Against the Ancients." *CEEC*, pp. 14–17. [1694.]

6 "Vindication of Paradise Lost." *CESC*, 3:198–200. [1694.]

*   *   *

7 HONORÉ, Jean. "Charles Gildon, rédacteur du *British Mercury* (1711–1712): Les attaques contre Pope, Swift et les wits." *EA*, 15(1962):347–64.

Joseph Glanvill

8 "From *An Essay Concerning Preaching*." *CESC*, 2:273–77. [1678.]

9 *Scepsis scientifica: or, Confest Ignorance, the Way to Science; in an Essay of the Vanity of Dogmatizing, and Confident Opinion*. 2 vols. in 1. London: E. Cotes for H. Eversden at the Greyhound in St. Paul's Churchyard, 1665. [For literary criticism see especially "Address to the Royal Society."]

Oliver Goldsmith

10 *The Beauties of English Poesy*. 2 vols. London, 1767.

11 *Collected Works*, ed. Arthur Friedman. 5 vols. Oxford: Clarendon P, 1966. [For literary criticism see especially "Essay on the Theatre; or, A Comparison Between Sentimental and Laughing Comedy," and those works cited separately in this bibliography.]

12 *An Enquiry into the Present State of Polite Learning in Europe*. London, 1759.

13 *Essays*. 2d ed. corrected. London: W. Griffin, 1766.

*   *   *

14 QUINTANA, Ricardo. *Oliver Goldsmith: A Georgian Study*. New York: Macmillan, 1967.*

15 ———. "Oliver Goldsmith as a Critic of the Drama." *SEL*, 5(1965):435–54.

Johann Christoph Gottsched

1 *Ausführliche Redekunst.* Leipzig: Breitkopf, 1743. [1736.]

2 *Versuch einer critischen Dichtkunst.* Leipzig, 1730.

3 *Versuch einer critischen Dichtkunst.* Darmstadt: Wissenschaftliche Buch-gesellschaft, 1962. [Photomech. repr. of the 5th ed., 1751.]

* * *

4 TISCH-WACKERNAGEL, J. Hermann. "Gottsched's Dramas Between Baroque and Enlightenment [Gottscheds dramatische Theorie und Praxis zwischen Barock und Aufklärung]." In *Proceedings of the Ninth Congress of the Australasian Universities' Languages and Literature Association, 19–26 August 1964,* ed. Marion Adams. Melbourne: U of Melbourne, 1964, pp. 120–22.

Gaspare Gozzi

5 "Difesa di Dante." In his *Letterati memorialisti e viaggiatori del settecento,* ed. E. Bonora. Milan, 1951. [1758.]

6 *Giudizio degli antichi poeti sopra la moderna censura di Dante.* Venice: Zatti, 1758.

George Granville

7 [Lord Lansdowne.] "Concerning Unnatural Flights in Poetry." In *The Laws of Poetry Explained and Illustrated,* ed. Charles Gildon. London, 1721, pp. 341–51. [1701.]

8 "An Essay upon Unnatural Flights in Poetry." *CESC,* 3:292–98.

Giovanni Vincenzo Gravina

9 *Della tragedia.* Venice: Geremia, 1731. [1715.]

10 *Prose,* pubblicate per cura di Paolo Emiliani-Giudici. Florence, 1857. [For literary criticism see especially "Discorso sopra *l'Endimione.*"]

11 *Ragion poetica.* Florence: Bastianelli, 1771. [1708.]

* * *

12 CARAMELLA, Santino. "Gravina e Vico." *Baretti,* 5, 27(1964):41–56.

13 CROCE, Benedetto. "L'Estetica del Gravina." In his *Problemi di estetica.* 4th ed. Bari: Laterza, 1948.

14 NANIA, Salvatore. *Il Gravina e il pensiero estetico russo nei saggi critici di Edgar Allan Poe: Il crollo di un mito.* Naples: Libreria Intercontinentalia, 1957.

Joseph Hall

1 [Bishop of Norwich.] *Characters of Vertves and Vices: In Two Books.* London: Bradwood for Edgar and Macham, 1608.

2 *Heaven upon Earth, and Characters of Vertues and Vices*, ed. Rudolf Kirk. New Brunswick, N.J.: Rutgers U P, 1948.

James Harris

3 *Three Treatises.* London: Nourse and Vaillant, 1744.

George Herbert

4 HUGHES, R. E. "George Herbert's Rhetorical World." *Criticism*, 3:86–94.

Johann Gottfried Herder

5 *Sämtliche Werke*, ed. B. Suphan and C. Redlich, et al. 33 vols. Berlin, 1877–1913. [For literary criticism see especially *Abhandlung über de. Ursprung der Sprache, Briefe zur Beförderung der Humanität, über die neuere deutsche Litteratur, vom Geist der ebräischen Poesie, über Bild, Dichtung, und Fabel.*]

* * *

6 CLARK, Robert T., Jr. *Herder: His Life and Thought.* Berkeley: U of California P, 1955.*

7 ———. "Herder's Conception of 'Kraft.' " *PMLA*, 57 (1942):737–52.

8 GILLIES, Alexander. *Herder und Ossian.* Berlin: Dünnhaupt, 1933.

9 MEINECKE, Friedrich. *Die Entstehung des Historismus.* 2 vols. Munich: R. Oldenbourg, 1936.* [See especially Vol. 2, pp. 383–479.]

10 NORDSIECK, Reinhold. "Herder: On the Natural History of Poetry." *TSL*, 7(1962):1–16.

11 SCHÜTZE, Martin. "The Fundamental Ideas in Herder's Thought." *MP*, 18(1920–21):65–78;121–302: 19(1921–22):113–30;361–82: 21(1923–24):29–48; 113–32.

12 ———. "J. G. Herder." *Monatshefte für den deutschen Unterricht*, 36(1944): 257–87.

13 STADELMANN, Rudolf. *Der historische Sinn bei Herder.* Halle: Niemeyer, 1928.

14 WEBER, Gottfried. *Herder und das Drama.* Weimar: Duncker, 1922.

Thomas Hobbes

15 "Answer to Davenant's Preface to *Gondibert.*" *GESC*, 2:54–67. [1650.]

1 *The Art of Rhetoric.* London: William Crooke at the Green Dragon without Temple-Bar, 1681.

2 *The English Works of Thomas Hobbes of Malmesbury,* ed. Sir William Molesworth. 11 vols. London: Bohm, 1839–45.

3 *Leviathan.* London, 1651. [For literary criticism see especially chap. 1–3.]

4 *Leviathan.* New York: Dutton, 1931. [Everyman's Library.] [WSP. W520]

5 "Preface to Homer." *CESC*, 2:67–76. [1675.]

* * *

6 ANCESCHI, Luciano. "Hobbes, Locke, e la 'discretion' della poesia." *RdE*, 6(1961):397–413.

7 THORPE, Clarence D. *Aesthetic Theory of Thomas Hobbes, with Special Reference to His Contribution to the Psychological Approach in English Literary Criticism.* Ann Arbor: U of Michigan P, 1940.

John Hughes

8 "An Essay on Allegorical Poetry." *CEEC*, pp. 86–104. [1715.]

9 "From 'Remarks on the *Fairy Queen.*' " *ECCE*, 1:301–4. [1715.]

10 "From 'Remarks on the *Shepherd's Calendar.*' " *ECCE*, 1:304–8.

11 "Of Style." *CEEC*, pp. 79–85. [1698.]

David Hume

12 *Essays and Treatises on Several Subjects.* Edinburgh, 1777.

13 *Essays Moral, Political and Literary.* London: Oxford U P, 1963.

14 *Four Dissertations: The Natural History of Religion; Of the Passions; Of Tragedy; Of the Standard of Taste.* London, 1757.

15 *Of the Standard of Taste, and Other Essays,* ed. John W. Lenz. Indianapolis: Bobbs-Merrill, 1965. [LLA84.]†

* * *

16 BRUNIUS, Teddy. *David Hume on Criticism.* Stockholm: Almqvist & Wiksell, 1952. [Studies Edited by the Institute of Art History, University of Uppsala.]

17 COHEN, Ralph. "David Hume's Experimental Method and the Theory of Taste." *ELH*, 25(1958):270–89.

18 ———. "The Transformation of Passion: A Study of Hume's Theories of Tragedy." *PQ*, 41(1962):450–64.

19 DIETL, Paul Joseph. "Explanation and Action: An Examination of the Controversy Between Hume and Some of His Contemporary Critics." *DA*, 26:5483–84 (Ind.).

20 DOERING, J. Frederick. "Hume and the Theory of Tragedy." *PMLA*, 52(1937):1130–4.

1   GARDINER, P. L. "Hume's Theory of the Passions." In *David Hume: A Symposium*, ed. D. F. Pears. London: Macmillan, 1963, pp. 31–42.

2   HIPPLE, Walter J. "The Logic of Hume's Essay 'of Tragedy.'" *PhQ*, 6(1956):43–52.

3   LANGLEY, Raymond Joseph. "Hume's Logic of the Imagination." *DA*, 26(1966):4003 (Fordham).

4   LINEBACK, Richard Harold. "The Place of the Imagination in Hume's Epistemology." *DA*, 24:2941 (Ind).

5   McGUINESS, Arthur Edward, Jr. "The Influence of David Hume's Critical Theory on Lord Kames's *Elements of Criticism*." *DA*, 25(1965):4127–28 (Wis).

6   MOSSNER, Ernest C. "Hume and the Ancient-Modern Controversy, 1725–52: A Study in Creative Skepticism." *University of Texas Studies in English*, 28(1949):139–53.

7   NOXON, James. "Hume's Opinions of Critics." *JAAC*, 20(1961):157–62.

8   SUGG, R. S., Jr. "Hume's Search for the Key with the Leathern Thong." *JAAC*, 16(1957):96–102.*

9   TAYLOR, Harold. "Hume's Theory of Imagination." *UTQ*, 22(1943): 180–90.

Bishop Richard Hurd

10   "A Dissertation on the Idea of Universal Poetry." *ECCE*, 2:860–71. [1766.]

11   *A Letter to Mr. Mason: On the Marks of Imitation.* Cambridge: Thurlbourne & Woodyer, 1757.

12   *Letters on Chivalry.* 2d ed. London: Millar, 1762.

13   *Letters on Chivalry and Romance by Richard Hurd (1762)*, ed. Hoyt Trowbridge. Los Angeles: Clark Memorial Library, U.C.L.A., 1963.

14   *The Works of Richard Hurd.* 8 vols. London, 1811.

*　　　*　　　*

15   CURRY, Stephen Jefferies. "The Literary Criticism of Richard Hurd." *DA*, 23(1962):2133–34 (Wis.).

16   ———. "Richard Hurd's Genre Criticism." *TSLL*, 8(1966):207–17.

17   HAMM, Victor M. "A Seventeenth-Century French Source for Hurd's *Letters on Chivalry and Romance*." *PMLA*, 52(1937):820–28.

18   MONTAGUE, Edwine. "Bishop Hurd's Association with Thomas Warton," *SSLL*, ed. Hardin Craig (1941), pp. 233–56.

19   SMITH, Audley L. "Richard Hurd's Letters on Chivalry and Romance." *ELH*, 6(1939):58–81.

20   TROWBRIDGE, Hoyt. "Bishop Hurd: A Reinterpretation." *PMLA*, 58(1943):450–65.

Francis Hutcheson

1 *Hibernicus's Letters: Or a Philosophical Miscellany.* 2d ed. London, 1734.

2 *An Inquiry into the Original of Our Ideas of Beauty and Virtue.* 5th ed. corr. London: Ware, 1753. [1725.]

*   *   *

3 FOWLER, Thomas. *Shaftesbury and Hutcheson.* London, 1882.

4 SCOTT, W. R. *Francis Hutcheson.* Cambridge: U P, 1900.

Tomás de Iriarte y Oropesa

5 *Fábulas literarias.* 3d ed. enl. Boston: Monroe, 1842. [1782.]

Samuel Johnson

6 *The Critical Opinions of Samuel Johnson,* ed. Joseph Epes Brown. Princeton: Princeton U P, 1926.

7 *The History of Rasselas, Prince of Abyssinia,* ed. G. B. Hill. Oxford: Clarendon, P 1960. [1759.]

8 *The Idler,* ed. Robert Lyam. London, 1827. [1758–60.] [The British Essayists, 20.] [For literary criticism see especially Nos. 60, 61, 77, 84.]

9 *Lives of the English Poets.* 2 vols. New York: Dutton, 1954. [Everyman's Library.]

10 "Preface to *The Plays of William Shakespeare.*" *ECCE,* 2:646–86. [1765.]

11 *The Rambler.* 4 vols. London: Dodsley, Owen, 1794. [1750–52.] [For literary criticism see especially Nos. 4, 36–37, 60, 86, 88, 90, 92, 93, 94, 121, 125, 139, 140, 143, 156, 158.]

12 *Samuel Johnson's Prefaces and Dedications,* ed. A. T. Hazen. New Haven: Yale U P, 1937.

13 *Selections from Dr. Johnson's "Rambler,"* ed. W. Hale White. Oxford: Clarendon P, 1907.

14 *The Yale Edition of the Works of Samuel Johnson,* ed. E. L. McAdam, Jr., with Donald and Mary Hyde. New Haven: Yale U P, 1958–64.

*   *   *

15 BABBITT, Irving. "Dr. Johnson and Imagination." *SWR* 13(1927):25–35.

16 BATE, Walter J. *The Achievement of Samuel Johnson.* New York: Oxford U P, 1955.

17 BOSWELL, James. See 66.1, 2.

18 BRONSON, Bertrand H. *Johnson Agonistes and Other Essays.* Berkeley: U of California P, 1946.

1   BROWN, Joseph E. *The Critical Opinions of Samuel Johnson.* Princeton: Princeton U P, 1926.

2   CLIFFORD, James Lowry. *Johnsonian Studies, 1887–1950: A Survey and Bibliography.* Minneapolis: U of Minnesota P, 1951.

3   CURRIE, H. MacL. "Johnson and the Classics." *NRam*, B, 17(1965):13–27.

4   DANIEL, Robert W. "Johnson on Literary Texture." In *Studies in Honor of John C. Hodges and Alwin Thaler*, ed. Richard B. Davis and John L. Lievsay. Knoxville: U of Tennessee P, 1961, pp. 57–65. [TSL, Special No.]

5   DELAUNE, Henry Malcolm. "An Examination of the Literary Prejudices of Dr. Samuel Johnson." *DA*, 22(1962):3643–44 (Tulane).

6   ———. "Johnson and the Matter of Imagination." *XUS*, 3:103–22.

7   DOWNES, Rackstraw. "Johnson's Theory of Language." *REL*, 3(1962): 29–41.

8   ELIOT, T. S. "Johnson as Critic and Poet." In his *On Poetry and Poets* London: Faber & Faber, 1957.

9   EVANS, Bergen. "Dr. Johnson's Theory of Biography." *RES*, 10(1934): 301–10.

10   GARDNER, Helen. "Johnson on Shakespeare." *NRam*, B, 17(1965):2–12.

11   HAGSTRUM, Jean H. "Johnson's Conception of the Beautiful, the Pathetic and the Sublime." *PMLA*, 64(1949):134–57.

12   ———. *Samuel Johnson's Literary Criticism.* Minneapolis: U of Minnesota P, 1952. [Phoenix–P268.]†

13   HAVENS, R. D. "Johnson's Distrust of the Imagination." *ELH*, 10(1939): 243–55.

14   HOUSTON, Percy H. *Dr. Johnson: A Study in Eighteenth-Century Humanism.* Cambridge, Mass.: Harvard U P, 1923.

15   KALLICH, Martin. "Samuel Johnson's Principles of Criticism and Imlac's 'Dissertation upon Poetry.'" *JAAC*, 25(1966):71–82.

16   KAUL, R. K. "Dr. Johnson on the Emotional Effect of Tragedy." *CaiSE*, 1963–66, pp. 203–11.

17   KEAST, William R. "Johnson's Criticism of the Metaphysical Poets." *ELH*, 17(1950):59–70.

18   ———. "The Theoretical Foundations of Johnson's Criticism." *C&C*, pp. 389–407.

19   LEAVIS, F. R. "Johnson and Augustanism." In his *The Common Pursuit*. New York: Stewart, 1952.

20   ———. "Johnson as Critic." *Scrutiny*, 12(1944):187–204.

21   MISENHEIMER, James Buford, Jr. "Samuel Johnson and the Didactic Aesthetic." *DA*, 25(1965):5934 (Colo).

22   MOWAT, John. "Samuel Johnson and the Critical Heritage of T. S. Eliot." *SGG*, 6(1964):231–47.

1 PERKINS, David. "Johnson on Wit and Metaphysical Poetry." *ELH*, 20(1953):200–17.

2 ROBERTS, Sydney Castle. *Doctor Johnson*. London: Duckworth, 1935.

3 ROSCOE, Edward Stanley. *Aspects of Dr. Johnson*. Cambridge: U P, 1928.

4 SACHS, Arieh. "Generality and Particularity in Johnson's Thought." *SEL*, 5(1965):491–511.

5 ———. "Johnson on Idle Solitude and Diabolic Imagination." *ES*, 48(1966): 180–89.

6 SHERBO, Arthur. *Samuel Johnson, Editor of Shakespeare*. Urbana, 1956. [ISLL, 42.]

7 SPITTAL, John Ker. *Contemporary Criticisms of Dr. Samuel Johnson*. London: Murray, 1923.

8 TATE, Allen. "Johnson on the Metaphysicals." *KR*, 11(1949):379–94.

9 TERRY, Charles Laymen. "Samuel Johnson and the Idea of Originality." *DA*, 27(1966):462A–463A (Mich).

10 WALKER, Isaac Newton. "Johnson's Criticism Criticized: The Contemporary View of Johnson's Later Reputation." *DA*, 27(1966):216A–217A (Texas).

11 WATKINS, Walter B. C. "Dr. Johnson on the Imagination: A Note." *RES*, 22(1946):131–34.

12 ———. *Johnson and English Poetry Before 1660*. Princeton: Princeton U P, 1936.

13 WATSON, Tommy G. "Johnson and Hazlitt on the Imagination in Milton." *SoQ*, 2(1964):123–33.

14 WESLING, Donald. "An Ideal of Greatness: Ethical Implications in Johnson's Critical Vocabulary." *UTQ*, 34(1965):133–45.

15 WIMSATT, William K., Jr. *The Prose Style of Samuel Johnson*. New Haven: Yale U P, 1941.

16 YOUNG, Karl. "Samuel Johnson on Shakespeare." *Wisconsin University Studies*, 18(1923).

Sir William Jones

17 "Essay on the Arts Commonly Called Imitative." In his *Poems Consisting Chiefly of Translations from the Asiatic Languages*. 2d ed. London, 1777.

18 "On the Arts Commonly Called Imitative." *ECCE*, 2:872–81. [1772.]

*   *   *

19 CANNON, Garland. "Sir William Jones and Dr. Johnson's Literary Club." *MP*, 63(1965):20–37.

Lord Kames

1   [Henry Home.] *Elements of Criticism.* 4th ed. Edinburgh, 1785. [1762.]

2   *"Elements of Criticism:* 'Emotions Caused by Fiction.' " *ECCE*, 2:838–47.

*   *   *

3   BEVILACQUA, Vincent M. "Lord Kames's Theory of Rhetoric." *SM*, 3(1963):309–27.

4   ———. "The Rhetorical Theory of Henry Home, Lord Kames." *DA*, 22:1742–42 (Ill).

5   BUNDY, Murray W. "Lord Kames and the Maggots in Amber." *JEGP*, 45(1946):199–208.

6   HORN, András. "Kames and the Anthropological Approach to Criticism." *PQ* 44(1965):211–33.

7   IRISH, Loomis Caryl. "Human Nature and the Arts: The Aesthetic Theory of Henry Home, Lord Kames," *DA*, 22:2832 (Colum).

8   McGUINNESS, Arthur Edward. See 80.5.

9   McKENZIE, Gordon. "Lord Kames and the Mechanist Tradition." UCDPE, 14(1943):93–121.

10 RANDALL, Helen W. *The Critical Theory of Lord Kames.* Northampton, Mass.: Smith College Studies in Modern Languages, 1944.

11 RICHARDS, I. A. "Metaphor." In his *The Philosophy of Rhetoric.* New York: Oxford U P, 1965.

Immanuel Kant

12 *Critique of Judgment*, trans. with analytical indexes by James Creed Meredith. Oxford: Clarendon P, 1964. [1790.]

*   *   *

13 CARRITT, Edgar F. "Addison, Kant and Wordsworth." *ESMEA*, 22(1937): 26–36.

14 HANDY, William J. *Kant and the Southern New Critics.* Austin: U of Texas P, 1963.

15 JAMES, David Gwilyn. *Skepticism and Poetry: An Essay on the Poetic Imagination.* London: Allen and Unwin, 1937.

16 MAUGHAM, W. Somerset. "Reflections on a Certain Book." In his *The Vagrant Mood.* New York: Doubleday, 1953.

Hippolyte de La Mesnardière

17 [Hippolyte Jules Dilet de La Mesnardière.] *La Poétique.* Paris: Sommaville, 1639.

Antoine de La Motte

18 [Antoine Houdar de La Motte.] *Discours sur Homère.* Paris, 1714.

1 *Odes: Avec un discours sur la poésie en général, et sur l'ode en particulier.* 2 vol. 3d ed. enl. Paris: Dupuis, 1711.

2 *Réflexions sur la critique.* Paris: Dupuis, 1715.

René le Bossu

3 *Monsieur Bossu's Treatise of the Epick Poem.* London: Knapton, 1719. [1675.]

4 "Selections from *The Treatise of the Epick Poem*," trans. "W.J." (London, 1695). *CM*, pp. 303–23.

5 *Traité du poëme épique.* Paris: Pralard, 1693.

Gottfried Leibniz

6 [Gottfried Wilhelm von Leibniz.] *Oeuvres philosophiques latines et françoises*, ed. Rud. Eric Raspe. Amsterdam and Leipzig: Schreuder, 1765. [For literary criticism see especially *Meditations de cognitione, veritate, et ideis*.]

* * *

7 KNEALE, William. "Leibniz and the Picture Theory of Language." *RIPh*, 20(1966):204–15.

Gotthold Ephraim Lessing

8 *Hamburgische Dramaturgie: Kritisch durchgesehene Gesamtausgabe mit Einleitung und Kommentar von Otto Mann.* 2d ed. Stuttgart: Kröner, 1963. [1767–69.]

9 *Laocoön: An Essay on the Limits of Painting and Poetry*, trans. Edward Allen McCormick. Indianapolis: Bobbs-Merrill, 1962. [LLA 78].

10 *Laokoön.* Berlin: Voss, 1766.

11 *Selected Prose Works*, trans. E. C. Beasley and H. Zimmern, ed. Edward Bell. New ed. rev. London: Bell, 1890.

* * *

12 BABBITT, Irving. *The New Laokoön: An Essay on the Confusion of the Arts.* Boston: Houghton Mifflin, 1910.

13 CLIVIO, Josef. *Lessing und der Problem das Tragödie.* Zurich: Münsterpresse, 1928. [Wege zur Dichtung, 5.]

14 JANET, Paul. "Histoire des doctrines esthétiques et littéraires en Allemagne: Lessing par E. Grucker." *JS* 1896, pp. 549–60; 1897, pp. 143–56, 271–84.

15 KOMMERELL, Max. See. 5.8.

16 NOLTE, Fred Otto. *Lessing's Laokoön.* Lancaster, Pa.: Lancaster P, 1940.

17 ROBERTSON, John George. *Lessing's Dramatic Theory.* Cambridge: U P, 1939.

18 WEDDIGEN, Otto. *Lessings Theorie der Tragödie.* Berlin, 1876.

John Locke

1 *An Essay Concerning the Understanding, Knowledge, Opinion and Assent,* ed. Benjamin Rand. Cambridge, Mass.: Harvard U P, 1931. [Hitherto unpublished draft dated 1671.]

2 MacLEAN, Kenneth. *John Locke and English Literature of the Eighteenth Century.* New Haven: Yale U P, 1936.

3 O'HARA, John Bryant. "John Locke's Philosophy of Discourse." *DA,* 23(1963):2625 (Okla).

Ignacio Luzán

4 *La Poética, o reglas de la poesía en general.* Madrid: De Sancha, 1789. [1737.]

5 *La Poética, o reglas de la poesía: Con un estudio por Luigi de Filippo.* 2 vols. Barcelona, n.p., 1956.

Jean-François Marmontel

6 *Éléments de littérature.* 3 vols. Paris, 1879.

7 *Oeuvres complètes de Marmontel.* 19 vols. New ed. Paris: Verdière, 1818–20.

8 *Poétique française.* 2 vols. Paris: Lesclapart, 1763.

Pietro Metastasio

9 [Pietro Antonio Domenico Buonaventura Metastasio.] *Opere del signor abate Pietro Metastasio.* XII: *Estratto dell' Arte poetica d'Aristotile, e considerazioni su la medesima.* Paris: Vedova Herissant, 1780–82.

*   *   *

10 DONDINI, Lucia. "Della fortuna di Orazio: L'Arte poetica tradotta e commentata dal Metastasio: II. Principi strutturali " *Rendiconti* (Istituto Lombardo), 96(1962):203–309.

11 GAVAZZENI, Franco. "Metastasio, lingua poetica e 'imitazione.'" *LM* 12(1962):503–12.

John Milton

12 *An Apology Against a Pamphlet Called "A Modest Confutation of the Animadversions upon the Remonstrant Against Smectymnuus,"* ed. Milford C. Jochums. Urbana: U of Illinois P, 1951.

13 *Complete Prose Works of John Milton,* ed. D. M. Wolfe. 4 vols. New Haven: Yale U P, 1953–66. [For literary criticism see especially "Apology for Smectymnuus," "Preface to *Paradise Lost,*" "Preface to *Paradise Regained,*" "Preface to *Samson Agonistes,*" "The Reason of Church Government."]

1   *Milton on Himself: Milton's Utterances upon Himself and His Work*, ed. John S. Diekhoff. 2d ed. New York: Humanities P, 1965.

2   *Prose Selections*, ed. Merritt Y. Hughes. New York: Odyssey P, 1947.

*   *   *

3   BLAU, Sheridan D. "Milton's Salvational Aesthetic." *JR*, 46(1966):282–95.

4   CLARK, Donald L. "John Milton and 'the Fitted Stile or Lofty, Mean, or Lowly.'" *SCN*, 11(1953):5–9. [Milton Society Supplement.]

5   ———. *John Milton at St. Paul's School: A Study of Ancient Rhetoric in English Renaissance Education*. New York: Columbia U P, 1948.

6   DIEKHOFF, John S. "The Function of the Prologue in *Paradise Lost*." *PMLA*, 57(1942):696–704.

7   DRAWVER, Pauline Sue. "Milton's Knowledge and Use of Aristotle." *DA*, 25:4684–85 (Ill).

8   DUHAMEL, P. A. "Milton's Alleged Ramism." *PMLA*, 67(1952):1035–53.

9   FLETCHER, Harris. *Contributions to a Milton Bibliography, 1800–1930*. Urbana: U of Illinois P, 1931.

10 FREEDMAN, Morris. See 73.5.

11 JEBB, Richard. "*Samson Agonistes* and the Hellenic Drama." *PBA*, 3(1908): 341–48.

12 KRANIDAS, Thomas. "Milton's Concept of Decorum." *DA*, 23(1963):4360 (Wash).

13 LANGDON, Ida. *Milton's Theory of Poetry and Fine Art*. New York: Russell and Russell, 1965. [1924.]

14 MUELLER, Martin. "Sixteenth-Century Italian Criticism and Milton's Theory of Catharsis." *SEL*, 6(1966):139–50.

15 MUIR, Kenneth. *John Milton*. New York: Longmans Green, 1955.

16 POLE, David. "Milton and Critical Method." *BJA*, 3(1963):245–58.

17 SCOTT, William O. "Ramism and Milton's Concept of Poetic Fancy." *PQ*, 42(1963):183–89.

18 STEVENS, David Harrison. *Reference Guide to Milton from 1800 to the Present Day*. Chicago: U of Chicago P, 1930.

19 THOMPSON, Elbert Nevius Sebring. *John Milton: A Topical Bibliography*. New Haven: Yale U P, 1916.

Jean Baptiste Molière

20 [Jean Baptiste Poquelin Molière.] MOORE, W. G. "Molière's Theory of Comedy." *ECr*, 6:137–44.

Corbyn Morris

1 *An Essay Towards Fixing the True Standards of Wit, Humour, Raillery, Satire and Ridicule.* London: Roberts, 1744.

2 *An Essay Towards Fixing the True Standards of Wit, Humour, Raillery, Satire and Ridicule.* Los Angeles: ARS, 1947. [No. X.]

*   *   *

3 TAVE, Stuart M. "Corbyn Morris: Falstaff, Humor and Comic Theory in the Eighteenth Century." *MP*, 50(1952):102–15.

Earl of Mulgrave

4 [John Sheffield, Duke of Buckingham and Normanby.] "An Essay upon Poetry." *CESC*, 2:286–96. [1682.]

Pierre Nicole

5 *Oeuvres.* Paris: Desprez, 1781.

6 "Of Comedy," trans. Clara W. Crane. *LC*, pp. 597–99. [1671.] [Selections.]

7 *Traité de la comédie*, ed. Georges Couton. Paris: Les Belles Lettres, 1962.

8 "Les Visionnaires," trans. Clara W. Crane. *LC*, p. 596. [1664.] [A selection.]

Francesco Pagano

9 [Francesco Mario Pagano.] "Discorso sull'origine e natura della poesia." In his *Opere filosofico-politiche ed estetiche.* Capolago, 1837.

Giuseppe Parini

10 "Dei principe delle belle lettere." In his *Prose*, ed. E. Bellorini. 2 vols. Bari: G. Laterza, 1913–15. [1773–75.]

11 *Poesie e prose, con apprendice di poeti satirici e didascalici del Settecento*, ed. Lanfranco Caretti. Milan: Ricciardi, 1951.

*   *   *

12 SPONGANO, Raffaele. *La Poetica del sensismo e la poesia del Parini.* Milan: Principato, 1933.

Henry Peacham

13 *The Complete Gentleman, The Truth of Our Times,* and *The Art of Living in London*, ed. Virgil B. Hetzel. Ithaca: Cornell U P, 1963 [Folger Documents of Tudor and Stuart Civilization.]

1 *"Of Poetry,* from *The Complete Gentleman." CESC,* 1:116–33. [1622.]

Edward Phillips

2 "Preface to *Theatrum Poetarum." CESC,* 2:256–72. [1675.]

Alexander Pope

3 "A Discourse on Pastoral Poetry." *ELC,* pp. 151–55. [1709.]

4 *Epistle to Arbuthnot.* London: Gilliver, 1734.

5 *Essay on Criticism.* London: Lewis, 1711.

6 "An Essay on Criticism." *GC,* pp. 386–404.

7 *"The Guardian,* No. 40: 'Pastoral Poetry.' " *ECCE,* 1:251–57. [1713.]

8 *Literary Criticism of Alexander Pope,* ed. Bertrand A. Goldgar. Lincoln: U of Nebraska P, 1965. [Bison. 403]

9 *Pastoral Poetry and An Essay on Criticism,* ed. E. Audra and Aubrey Williams. New Haven: Yale U P, 1961. [Twickenham edition of the Poems of Alexander Pope, Vol. I.]

10 " 'Preface of the Editor' to *The Works of Shakespeare." ECCE,* 1:278–90. [1725.]

11 "Preface to the Translation of the *Iliad." CEEC,* pp. 323–52. [1715.]

12 "Postscript to the Translation of the *Odyssey." ECCE,* 1:291–300. [1726.]

13 *Works of Pope,* ed. W. Elwin and W. J. Courthope. 10 vols. London, 1871–89.

*   *   *

14 ADEN, John M. "The Doctrinal Design of *An Essay on Criticism." CE,* 22:311–15.

15 ADLER, Jacob H. "Pope and the Rules of Prosody." *PMLA,* 76(1961): 218–26.

16 ALLEN, Robert J. "Pope and the Sister Arts." In *Pope and His Contemporaries: Essays Presented to George Sherburn,* ed. J. Clifford and L. A. Landa. Oxford: Clarendon P, 1949, pp. 78–88.

17 CURTIS, Penelope. "Pope the Good Augustan." *MCR,* 7 (1964):34–48.

18 GOLDGAR, Bertrand A. "Pope's Theory of the Passions: The Background of Epistle II of the *Essay on Man." PQ,* 41:730–43.

1 HUSEBOE, Arthur Robert. "Pope's Critical Views of the London Stage."
RECTR, 3(1964):25–37.

2 MACK, Maynard. *Essential Articles for the Study of Alexander Pope.*
Hamden, Conn.: Archon, 1964.

3 ———. " 'Wit and Poetry and Pope': Some Observations on His Imagery."
In *Pope and His Contemporaries: Essays Presented to George Sherburn*, ed.
J. L. Clifford and L. A. Landa. Oxford, 1949, pp. 20–44.

4 MARESCA, Thomas E. "Pope's Defense of Satire: The First Satire of the
Second Book of Horace, Imitated." *ELH*, 31(1964):366–94.

5 NIXON, Howard Kenneth. "The Literary Theories of Alexander Pope."
DA, 22:1614–15 (Ill).

6 ROOT, Robert Kilburn. *The Poetical Career of Alexander Pope.* Princeton:
Princeton U P, 1938.

7 SANDERS, Charles. "Toward a Definition of Nature in Pope's *Essay on
Criticism*." *DA*, 26(1965):2728–29 (Mich).

8 STEIN, William Bysshe. "Pope's *An Essay on Criticism*: The Play of Sophia."
BuR, 13(1965):75–86.

9 SULLIVAN, J. P., ed. "Alexander Pope on Classics and Classicists." *Arion*,
5(1966):235–53.

10 WARREN, Austin. *Alexander Pope as Critic and Humanist.* Princeton:
Princeton U P, 1929.

11 ———. "The Mask of Pope." *SR*, 54(1946):19–33.

12 WARTON, Joseph. See 98.14.

Manuel José Quintana

13 *Obras ineditas del excmo. señor d. Manuel José Quintana*, ed. M. Cañete.
Madrid: Medina y Navarro, 1872.

14 "Las Reglas del drama, ensayo didáctico." In his *Poesías de d. Manuel Josef
Quintana*. 2 vols. 3d ed. enl. and rev. Madrid: Imprenta Nacional, 1821.
[1791.]

* * *

15 TOMÉ, Eustaquio. "Manuel José Quintana: Ensayo de crítica literaria."
BFM, 9(1962):57–127.

Jean Racine

16 *Five Plays*, trans. Kenneth Muir. New York: Hill and Wang, 1960. [For
literary criticism see especially the prefaces to the dramatic works.]

17 *Oeuvres complètes*, ed. Raymond Picard. Paris: Gallimard, 1960. [For
literary criticism see especially Vol. 2, "Prose."]

18 *Principes de la tragédie en marge de la Poétique d'Aristote*, ed. Eugène Vinaver.
Manchester: University of Manchester, 1951.

* * *

1 HALEY, Marie Philip. *Racine and the Art Poétique of Boileau.* Baltimore: Johns Hopkins P, 1938.

Allan Ramsay

2 "Preface to *The Ever Green.*" *CEEC*, pp. 399–402. [1724.]

René Rapin

3 *Comparison des poëmes d'Homere et de Virgile.* 3rd ed. rev. and enl. Paris: Barbin, 1664 (1674?). [1667.]

4 *De Carmine Pastorali, Prefixed to Thomas Creech's Translation of the Idylliums of Theocritus.* Ann Arbor: ARS, 1947.

5 *Reflections on Aristotle's Treatise of Poesie*, trans. Thomas Rymer. London, 1674.

6 *Reflections on Aristotle's Treatise of Poesie.* Chicago: Newberry Library, 1960.

7 *Reflections upon the Use of the Eloquence of These Times, Together with a Comparison Between the Eloquence of Cicero and Demosthenes*, "translated out of French." Oxford, 1672.

8 *Les Réflexions sur l'eloquence, la poétique, l'histoire et la philosophie.* Rev. and corrected ed. Amsterdam: Wolfgang, 1686.

9 *Réflexions sur la poétique d'Aristote.* 1674. [French.]

10 *The Whole Critical Works of Monsieur Rapin*, trans. several hands. 2 vols. London: Bonwicke, 1706.

Sir Joshua Reynolds

11 *Fifteen Discourses Delivered in the Royal Academy.* New York: Dutton, 1907. [Everyman's Library.]

12 "*The Idler*, No. 76: 'False Criticisms of Painting.'" *ECCE*, 2:829–33. [1759.]

13 "*The Idler*, No. 82: 'The True Idea of Beauty.'" *ECCE*, 2:834–37. [1759.]

14 *Works of Sir Joshua Reynolds*, ed. Edmund Malone. 3d ed. rev. London, 1801.

*   *   *

15 BATE, Walter Jackson. "Johnson and Reynolds: The Premise of General Nature." See 52.11.

92

1   ELLIOTT, Eugene Clinton. "Reynolds and Hazlitt." *JAAC*, 21(1962):73–79.

2   HILLES, F. W. *The Literary Career of Sir Joshua Reynolds*. Cambridge: U P, 1936.

3   ———. "Sir Joshua's Prose." In his *The Age of Johnson*. New Haven: Yale U P, 1949.

4   HIPPLE, Walter J., Jr. "General and Particular in the *Discourses* of Sir Joshua Reynolds: A Study in Method." *JAAC*, 11(1953):231–47.

5   MACKLEM, Michael. "Reynolds and the Ambiguities of Neo-Classical Criticism." *PQ*, 31(1952):383–98.

6   TEMPLEMAN, W. D. "Sir Joshua Reynolds on the Picturesque." *MLN*, 47(1932):446–48.

7   THOMPSON, Elbert N. S. "The *Discourses* of Sir Joshua Reynolds." *PMLA*, 32(1917):339–66.

8   TROWBRIDGE, Hoyt. "Platonism and Sir Joshua Reynolds." *ES*, 21(1939):1–7.

Samuel Richardson

9   BALL, Donald Lewis. "Samuel Richardson's Theory of Fiction." *DA*, 26(1966):3943 (NC).

10   CARROLL, John. "Richardson on Pope and Swift." *UTQ*, 33(1963):19–29.

Vincente de los Ríos

11   *Análisis del Quijote*. Barcelona: Gorchs, 1834. [1780.]

Jean Jacques Rousseau

12   *Lettre à D'Alembert sur les spectacles*. Paris: Garnier, 1926. [1758.]

13   *Oeuvres complètes*. II: *La Nouvelle Héloïse, Théâtre, Poésies, Essais littéraires*. Ed. Bernard Guyon, Jacques Cherer, and Charly Guyot. Paris: Gallimard, 1961. [Bibliothèque de la Pléiade.]

* * *

14   DÉDÉYAN, Charles. *Rousseau et la sensibilité littéraire à la fin du 18ième siècle*. Paris: Centre de Documentation Universitaire, 1963.*

15   MAY, Georges. "Rousseau's Literary Writings: An Important New Edition." *MLN*, 67(1962):519–28.

16   MONTY, Jeanne R. "The Criticism of Rousseau in the *Correspondance Littéraire*." *MLQ*, 24(1963):99–103.

Thomas Rymer

1 *The Critical Works of Thomas Rymer*, ed. Curt A. Zimansky. New Haven: Yale U P, 1956.

2 "Preface to Rapin." *CESC*, 2:163–81. [1674.]

3 *A Short View of Tragedy*. London: Baldwin, 1693.

4 *The Tragedies of the Last Age*. 2d ed. London: Baldwin, 1692. [1678.]

*   *   *

5 BUTLER, Samuel. "Upon Critics Who Judge of Modern Plays Precisely by the Rules of the Ancients." *CESC*, 2:278–81.

6 DUTTON, George B. "The French Aristotelian Formalists and Thomas Rymer." *PMLA*, 29(1914):152–88.

7 WALCOTT, Fred G. "John Dryden's Answer to Thomas Rymer's *The Tragedies of the Last Age*." *PQ*, 15(1936):194–214.

Saint-Évremond

8 [Charles de Marguetel de Saint Denis.] *Critique littéraire*. Paris: Bossard, 1921.

9 "Letter to the Duchess of Mazarin," trans. Mr. des Maizeaux. *LC*, pp. 665–66. [1678.]

10 *Miscellanea: Or Various Discourses*, trans. F. Spence. London: Holford, 1686.

11 *Oeuvres en prose*, ed. René Ternois. 2 vols. Paris: Didier, 1963–65.

12 "Of the Imitation of the Ancients," trans. Mr. des Maizeaux. *LC*, pp. 663–65. [1678.] [Selections.]

13 "Of Tragedy, Ancient and Modern," trans. Mr. des Maizeaux. *LC*, pp. 659–63. [1672.] [Selections.]

14 *Les Veritables oeuvres de M. de Saint-Évremond*. 3 vols. London, 1705.

15 *Works*, trans. Mr. des Maizeaux. 3 vols. London, 1728.

*   *   *

16 HOPE, Quentin M. *Saint-Évremond: The "Honnête Homme" as Critic*. Bloomington: Indiana U P, 1962. [IUPHS, 51.]

Georges de Scudéry

17 "The Preface to *Ibrahim*," trans. Clara W. Crane. *LC*, pp. 580–85. [1641.] [Selections.]

1 *Works.* Paris, 1641. [For literary criticism see especially "Observations" on *Le Cid.*]

Madeleine de Scudéry

2 *Conversations nouvelles de la poésie françoise jusqu'a Henri IV.* N.p., 1684.

Earl of Shaftesbury

3 [Anthony Ashley Cooper.] *Characteristics of Men, Manners, Opinions, Times.* 2d ed. London, 1714.

4 *Characteristics of Men, Manners, Opinions, Times, etc.*, ed. J. M. Robertson. 2 vols. London, 1900. [For literary criticism see especially "A Letter Concerning Enthusiasm," "*Sensus Communis:* An Essay on the Freedom of Wit and Humor," "Soliloquy: Or Advice to An Author," "The Moralists, a Philosophical Rhapsody," "Miscellaneous Reflections on the Preceding Treatises."]

5 "From *Characteristics of Men, Manners, Opinions, Times.*" *ECCE*, 1:164–228. [1711.]

* * *

6 ALDERMAN, William E. "Shaftesbury and the Doctrine of Moral Sense in the Eighteenth Century." *PMLA*, 46(1931):1087–94.

7 ALDRIDGE, A. O. "Lord Shaftesbury and the Test of Truth." *PMLA*, 60(1945):129–56.

8 ———. "Lord Shaftesbury's Literary Theories." *PQ*, 24(1945):46–64.

9 BRETT, R. L. *The Third Earl of Shaftesbury: A Study in Eighteenth-Century Literary Theory.* New York: Hutchinson, 1951.

10 MARSH, Robert. "Shaftesbury's Theory of Poetry: The Importance of 'Inward Colloquy.' " *ELH*, 28:54–69.

11 MOORE, Cecil A. "The Return to Nature in English Poetry of the Eighteenth Century." *MP*, 14(1917):243–91.

12 ———. "Shaftesbury and the Ethical Poets in England, 1700–1760." *PMLA*, 31(1916):264–325.

13 SIMON, Irene. "Shaftesbury and Eighteenth-Century Poetry." *RLV*, 27:200–15.

14 STOLNITZ, Jerome. "On the Significance of Lord Shaftesbury in Modern Aesthetic Theory." *PhQ*, 11(1961):97–113.

15 TUVESON, Ernest. "The Importance of Shaftesbury." *ELH*, 20(1953):267–99.

16 ———. "The Origins of 'Moral Sense.' " *HLQ*, 11(1948):241–59.

Adam Smith

17 *Essays Philosophical and Literary.* London: Ward, Lock, 1880. [The World Library of Standard Works.]

1 *Lectures on Rhetoric and Belles Lettres Delivered at the University of Glasgow, Reported by a Student*, ed. John M. Lothian. New York: Nelson, 1963. [1762–63.]

* * *

2 BEVILACQUA, Vincent M. "Adam Smith's *Lectures on Rhetoric and Belles Lettres.*" *SSL*, 3(1965):41–60.

3 LOTHIAN, John M. "Adam Smith as a Critic of Shakespeare." *Papers, Mainly Shakespearean*, ed. G. I. Duthie. Edinburgh: Oliver Boyd, 1964, pp. 1–9. [U of Aberdeen Studies, 147.]

4 ZALL, Paul M. "Adam Smith as Literary Critic?" *BNYPL*, 70(1966):265–69.

Giuseppe Spalletti

5 *Saggio sopra la bellezza.* Florence: Olschki, 1933. [1765.]

Richard Steele

6 "*Guardian* XII: 'On Critics.' " *CEEC*, pp. 293–97. [1713.]

7 "*Tatler* LXVIII: 'Shakespeare.' " *CEEC*, pp. 289–92. [1709.]

Laurence Sterne

8 JEFFERSON, D. W. "Tristram Shandy and the Tradition of Learned Wit." *EIC*, 1(1951):239, 244–45.

9 MacLEAN, Kenneth. "Imagination and Sympathy: Sterne and Adam Smith." *JHI*, 10(1949):399–410.

Percival Stockdale

10 *Inquiry into the Nature and Genuine Laws of Poetry, Including a Particular Defense of the Writings, and Genius of Mr. Pope.* London: Conant, 1778.

11 *Lectures on the Truly Eminent English Poets.* London: Shury, 1807.

Jonathan Swift

12 *The Complete Works of Swift.* 6 vols. London: Greening, 1906–8.

13 *A Tale of a Tub, Written for the Universal Improvement of Mankind: To which is added An Account of a Battle Between the Ancient and Modern Books in St. James' Library.* London, 1704.

1 *A Tale of a Tub, to which is added The Battle of the Books, and The Mechanical Operation of the Spirit*, ed. A. C. Guthkelch and D. Nichol Smith. 2d ed. Oxford: Clarendon P, 1958.

*   *   *

2 BEAUMONT, Charles Allen. *Swift's Classical Rhetoric*. Athens: U of Georgia P, 1961. [Repr. from *UGM*.]

3 SCRUGGS, Charles Watkins. "The Bee and the Spider: Swift's Aesthetic and His Role as a Literary Critic." *DA*, 26(1966):5417–18 (Wis).

Sir William Temple

4 "Of Poetry." *CESC*, 3:73–109. [1690.]

5 *Sir William Temple's Essay on Ancient and Modern Learning and on Poetry*, ed. J. E. Spingarn. Oxford: Clarendon P, 1909.

6 *Three Essays*. Bombay and Calcutta: Indian Branch, Oxford U P, 1939. [For literary criticism see especially "Of Poetry."]

Jean Terrasson

7 *Dissertation critique sur l'Iliade d'Homère*. Paris: Fournier and Coustelier, 1715.

Lewis Theobald

8 "*The Censor*, No. 10: '*King Lear*.'" *ECCE*, 1:309–13. [1715.]

9 "*The Censor*, No. 36: 'The Character of Tragic Heroes.'" *ECCE*, 1:313–16. [1717.]

10 "*The Censor*, No. 70: '*Julius Caesar*.'" *ECCE*, 1:316–19. [1717.]

James Thomson

11 *The Seasons*. London, 1730.

12 *Seasons*. London: Nonesuch P, 1927.

*   *   *

13 COHEN, Ralph. *The Art of Discrimination: Thomson's "The Seasons" and the Language of Criticism*. Berkeley: U of California P, 1964.

14 ———. "Literary Criticism and Artistic Interpretation: Eighteenth-Century Illustrations of *The Seasons*." In *Reason and the Imagination: Studies in the History of Ideas, 1600–1800*, ed. J. A. Mazzeo. New York: Columbia U P, 1962, pp. 279–306.

Joseph Trapp

1 *Lectures on Poetry Read in the Schools of Natural Philosophy at Oxford*, trans. William Bowyer and William Clarke, ed. William Bowyer. London: Hitch and Davis, 1942.

2 "*Lectures on Poetry:* 'Of the Beauty of Thought in Poetry; or of Elegance and Sublimity.' " *ECCE*, 1:229–50. [1711, 1715, 1719.]

3 *Praelectiones poeticae in Schola naturalis philosophiae Oxon habitae.* 2d ed. London: Lintott and Bowyer, 1722. [29 lectures.]

Giambattista Vico

4 *The New Science of Giambattista Vico*, ed. and trans. T. G. Bergin and M. H. Fisch. Rev. trans. of 3d ed. [1744]. Ithaca: Cornell U P, 1968.

5 *La Scienza nuova*, ed. Paolo Rossi. 2 vols. 2d ed. of 1744. Milan: Rizzoli, 1963.

*   *   *

6 AMERIO, Franco. *Introduzione allo studio di G. B. Vico.* Turin: Società Editrice Internazionale, 1947.

7 AUERBACH, Erich. "Vico and Aesthetic Historicism." In his *Scenes from the Drama of European Literature.* New York: Meridian, 1959.

8 BERLIN, Isaiah. "The Philosophical Ideas of Giambattista Vico." In *Art and Ideas in Eighteenth Century Italy.* Rome: Ed. di Storia e Letteratura, 1960, pp. 156–233. [Lectures given at the Italian Institute, 1957–58.]

9 CROCE, Benedetto. *La Filosofia de Giambattista Vico.* 6th ed. Bari: Laterza, 1962.*

10 ——, and Fausto NICOLINI. *Bibliografia* Vichiano. 2 vols. Naples: Ricciardi, 1947.

11 FUBINI, Mario. *Stile e umantià di Giambattista Vico.* Bari: Laterza, 1946.

12 LANZA, Franco. *Saggi di poetica vichiana.* Varese: Magenta, 1961.

13 MARIN, Demetrio. "Estetica antica ed estetica moderna." Annotated. *APh*, 3(1964):221–35.

14 TAGLIACOZZO, Giorgio, and Hayden V. WHITE. *Giambattista Vico: An International Symposium.* Baltimore: Johns Hopkins U P, 1969.

Voltaire

15 [François Marie Arouet.] *Critical Essays on Dramatic Poetry.* London: Davis and Reymers, 1761. [English.]

16 *Dissertations sur le théâtre.* Heidelberg: Winter, 1949.

17 *An Essay Upon the Civil Wars of France, Extracted from Curious Manuscripts . . . and also Upon the Epick Poetry of the European Nations from Homer Down to Milton.* London: Jallason, 1727.

1   *Oeuvres complètes*, ed. Louis Moland. 52 vols. Paris: Garnier, 1877–83.
    [For literary criticism see especially "Commentaires sur Corneille," "Discours
    sur la tragédie," "Dissertations sur la tragédie ancienne et moderne," "Essai
    sur la poésie epique," "Lettre à l'Académie français," "Preface à *Oedipe*,"
    "Le Siècle de Louis XIV," and those works cited separately in this bibliog-
    raphy.]

2   *Remarques sur le Pensées de M. Pascal*, ed. Raymond Naves. Paris: Garnier,
    1951.

3   *Rhétorique et poétique de Voltaire*. Paris: Johanneau, 1828.

4   *Le Temple du goût*, ed. E. Carcassonne. Paris: Société des Textes Français
    Modernes 1938.

5   *Voltaire's Essay on Epic Poetry: A Study and an Edition*, ed. Florence Donnell
    White. Albany, N.Y.: Brandow, 1915.

*   *   *

6   LION, Henri. *Les Tragédies et les théories dramatiques de Voltaire*. Paris,
    1895.

7   LOUNSBURY, Thomas Raynesford. *Shakespeare and Voltaire*. New York:
    Scribner, 1902.

8   MERIAN-GENAST, Ernst. "Voltaire und die Entwicklung der Idée der
    Weltliteratur." *RF*, 40(1927):1–226.

9   NAVES, Raymond. *Le Goût de Voltaire*. Paris: Garnier, 1938.

10 RAMSEY, Warren. "Voltaire and Homer." *PMLA*, 66(1951):182–96.

11 TROUSSON, R. "Poète et poésie selon Voltaire." *NS*, 12(1963):543–54.

Joseph Warton

12 "*The Adventurer*, Nos. 75, 80: 'The Odyssey.'" *ECCE*, 2:704–13.

13 "*The Adventurer*, No. 101: 'Milton.'" *ECCE*, 2:713–17.

14 *An Essay on the Writings and Genius of Pope*. London: Cooper, 1756.

15 *Essay on the Genius and Writings of Pope*. 5th ed. corrected. London:
    Richardson, 1806.

16 "From *An Essay on the Genius and Writings of Pope*." *ECCE*, 2:717–63.

*   *   *

17 ALLISON, James. "Joseph Warton's Reply to Dr. Johnson's *Lives*." *JEGP*,
    51(1952):186–91.

18 GOSSE, Edmund William. *Two Pioneers of Romanticism: Joseph and Thomas
    Warton*. London: Proceedings of the British Academy, 1915–16.

19 LEEDY, Paul F. "Genres Criticism and the Significance of Warton's *Essay
    on Pope*." *JEGP*, 45(1946):140–46.

1 MacCLINTOCK, W. D. *Joseph Warton's "Essay on Pope": A History of the Five Editions.* Chapel Hill: U of North Carolina P, 1933.

2 MORLEY, Edith J. "Joseph Warton: A Comparison of His *Essay on the Genius and Writings of Pope* with His Edition of Pope's *Works.*" *E&S,* 9(1924):98–114.

3 SCHICK, George B. "Joseph Warton's Critical Essays in His *Virgil.*" *N&Q,* 8:255–56.

4 TROWBRIDGE, Hoyt. "Joseph Warton on the Imagination." *MP,* 35(1937):73–87.

5 ———. "Joseph Warton's Classification of English Poets." *MLN,* 51(1936): 515–18.

Thomas Warton

6 "From *Observations on the Fairy Queen.*" *ECCE,* 2:764–86. [1754.]

7 *The History of English Poetry, from the Close of the Eleventh to the Commencement of the Eighteenth Century.* London: Dodsley, 1774.

8 *A History of English Poetry: An Unpublished Continuation,* ed. Rodney M. Baine. Los Angeles: William Andrews Clark Memorial Library, U of California, 1953. [ARS, 39.]

9 *Observations on the "Fairy Queen" of Spenser.* 2d ed. corrected and enl. London: Dodsley, 1762.

10 *Warton's History of English Poetry,* ed. David Nichol Smith. London: Milford, 1929.

*   *   *

11 GOSSE, Edmund William. See 98.18.

12 HAVENS, Raymond D. "Thomas Warton and the Eighteenth-Century Century Dilemma." *SP,* 25(1928):36–50.

13 KINGHORN, A. M. "Warton's *History* and Early English Poetry." *ES,* 44(1963):197–204.

Isaac Watts

14 *Horae Lyricae.* London, 1706.

15 "Preface to *Horae Lyricae.*" *ECCE,* 1:148–63.

*   *   *

16 LEICESTER, James H. "Dr. Johnson and Isaac Watts." *NRam,* B, 15(1964): 2-10.

17 STEESE, Peter B. "Dennis' Influence on Watts's Preface to *Horae Lyricae.*" *PQ,* 42(1963):275–77.

Leonard Welsted

18 "Dissertation Concerning the State of Poetry." *CEEC,* pp. 355–95. [1794.]

Bishop John Wilkins

1 *Essay Towards a Real Character and a Philosophical Language.* London: Gellibrand, 1668.

Johann Joachim Winckelmann

2 *Gedanken über die Nachahmung der griechischen Werke in Malerey und Bildhauerkunst.* Friedrichstadt, 1755.

3 *Gedanken über die Nachahmung der griechischen Werke in Malerey und Bildhauerkunst.* Heibronn: Henninger, 1885.

4 *Geschichte der Kunst des Altertums.* Dresden, 1764. [*The History of Ancient Art Among the Greeks*, trans. G. H. Lodge. 2 vols. Boston: Osgood, 1880.

5 *Winckelmanns kleine Schriften zur Geschichte der Kunst des Altertums*, ed. Hermann Uhde-Bernays. Leipzig, 1913.

* * *

6 HATFIELD, Henry C. *Winckelmann and His German Critics, 1755–1781.* New York: Columbia U P, 1943.

7 KREUZER, Ingrid. *Studien zu Winckelmanns Aesthetik: Normativität und historisches Bewusstsein.* Berlin: Akademic, 1959.

8 SCHULTZ, Franz. *Klassik und Romantik der Deutschen.* 2 vols. Stuttgart: Metzler, 1935. [See especially "Winckelmann und sein Wirkung," "'Klassik' und 'Klassizismus.'"]

Robert Wood

9 *Essay on the Original Genius and Writings of Homer.* London: Hughs, 1775. [1769.]

Edward Young

10 *Conjectures on Original Composition.* London: Millar, 1759.

11 *Conjectures on Original Composition*, ed. Edith Morley. New York: Longmans Green, 1918.

12 "On Lyric Poetry." *ECCE*, 1:410–15. [1728.]

* * *

13 KELLY, Richard M. "Imitation of Nature: Edward Young's Attack upon Alexander Pope." *XUS*, 4(1965):168–76.

1 McKILLOP, A. D. "Richardson, Young and the *Conjectures.*" *MP*, 22(1925):391–411.

2 STEINKE, M. W. *Edward Young's "Conjectures on Original Composition" in England and Germany.* New York: Stechert, 1917.

Francesco Zanotti

3 [Francesco Maria Zanotti.] *Discorsi e orazioni.* Venice: Alvisopoli, 1830. [For literary criticism see especially "Discorso intorno alle poesie dell' ab. Golt ed. agli aromenti del più bel poetare," "Discorso dello stile in generale e della purità e proprietà della lingua."]

NOTES

INDEX

INDEX

INDEX

INDEX

INDEX

INDEX

INDEX